Our Workshop & *The Lathe And How To Use It*
1866 - 1867

By
Temple Thorold

Toolemera Press
History Preserved
toolemerapress.com

Our Workshop & The Lathe And How To Use It: 1866 - 1867
by Temple Thorold

Originally published by George Routledge And Sons, London and New York

No part of this book may be reproduced, stored in an electronic retrieval system, or transmitted in any form or by any means, electronic, photocopy, photographic or otherwise without the written permission of the publisher.

Excerpts of one page or less for the purpose of review and comment are permissible.

Copyright © 2019 Gary Roberts DBA Toolemera Press
All rights reserved

International Standard Book Number
ISBN: 9781087819426

Published by Gary Roberts DBA Toolemera Press
Wilmington, North Carolina 28401 USA

Manufactured by IngramSpark

www.toolemerapress.com

"It is our intention to notice many things, however trivial, that may in any way serve to enlighten our readers respecting the joiner's art."

Offered now for the first time as one book, *Our Workshop* & *The Lathe And How To Use It* are the only known works of Temple Thorold. Written with a directness and clarity seldom found in nineteenth century craft books, *Our Workshop* & *The Lathe And How To Use It* represent an invaluable resource for the modern traditional woodworker as well as the educator interested in applying the practices of Slojd to classwork.

Published by George Routedge in *Every Boys Annual*, London and New York, *Our Workshop* was offered first as a serial and then in book form in 1866. *The Lathe And How To Use It,* was published in serialized form in 1867. Together, these two titles offer the modern traditional woodworker an expansive and period correct introduction to traditional hand tool woodworking and lathe work.

Temple Thorold wrote to the "amateur" in hand work, a 19th century term applied to socially approved craft activities of the middle and upper classes. It is worth noting that during this time period, the theories and applications of Slojd were introduced throughout Europe and Great Britain. Sloyd is the theory of hand work as a necessary component of educational development. Sloyd was developed and introduced by Uno Cygnaeus of Finland in 1865 and popularized by Otto Salomon in his influential 1891 text *The Teacher's Hand-Book Of Slojd*, available from the Toolemera Press at most book stores. ISBN: 9780983150091.

Who Temple Thorold was, is yet unkown. It is likely that Temple Thorold was an Anglican churchman who wrote under a pen name. It was common practice for both Churchmen and the upper classes of British society to publish under pen names. James Lukin, an Anglican Deacon, initially published his amateur craft books as "A Practical Mechanic". The Thorold family originated as a Viking family from Malmo, Sweden who arrived in Great Britain in the early 10th century. A prosperous family that included Barons, Baronets, and Churchmen, the Thorolds owned substantial tracks of land in Lincolnshire. Since 1380, Marston Hall has been the seat of the Thorold family.

Gary Roberts, Publisher of the TOOLEMERA PRESS, returns to print classic books on early crafts, trades and industries, from his personal collection.

Table Of Contents

Our Workshop

1. Carpentry And Joinery
2. The Bench
3. How To Use The Tools
4. Remarks On The Seasoning And Choice Of The Woods
5. Various Methods Of Joining Timber
6. Simple Works In Wood
7. Grooving Planes, Etc.
8. Mortising And Tenoning
9. Dovetailing
10. Venering
11. Varnishing And French Polishing

The Lathe And How To Use It

1. The Lathe
2. Chucks, Etc.
3. Hand-Turning Tools
4. First Practice
5. Sharpening Tools
6. Hardwood Turning
7. On The Choice Of Materials

OUR WORKSHOP;

BEING

A PRACTICAL GUIDE TO THE AMATEUR

IN

THE ART OF CARPENTRY AND JOINERY.

PROFUSELY ILLUSTRATED.

NEW YORK:
GEORGE ROUTLEDGE AND SONS,
416, BROOME STREET.
1866.

CONTENTS.

CHAP.		PAGE
	CARPENTRY AND JOINERY...	1
I.	THE BENCH	6
II.	HOW TO USE THE TOOLS...	13
III.	REMARKS ON THE SEASONING AND CHOICE OF THE WOODS	53
IV.	VARIOUS METHODS OF JOINING TIMBER	66
V.	SIMPLE WORKS IN WOOD	75
VI.	GROOVING PLANES, ETC.	129
VII.	MORTISING AND TENONING	147
VIII.	DOVETAILING	165
IX.	VENEERING	180
X.	VARNISHING AND FRENCH POLISHING	187

OUR WORKSHOP.

CARPENTRY AND JOINERY.

WE are sorry to be obliged to admit, that to enter into a scientific investigation of the mechanical principles on which the art of Carpentry depends, would be worse than useless. By so doing, we should only be occupying valuable space, without imparting instruction, or affording pleasure to many of our readers.

We should fail in the first, simply because *amateurs* would not peruse such unpalatable matter; for so it would be considered by the every-day reader of light literature. The latter, or pleasure-seeker, would ask why we did not tell him how to make some ornamental or useful article, instead of delivering a dry lecture on the *composition* and *resolution of forces*, the strengths of different forms of beams, and many other matters which are all-important to the practical carpenter. In truth, there always has been, and we fear there always must be, a very wide distinction between the *practical* and the *amateur* mechanic.

While the former is dependent on the correct scientific principles of his art, to enable him to guard against the most disastrous consequences, the latter is quite satisfied with a mere superficial knowledge, sufficient to enable him to carry trifling matters to a successful issue.

Carpentry is one of the most interesting and useful branches of mechanical art. It is also a cleanly and healthy employment. That carpentry is popular amongst boys, no one will deny. Who ever saw a youngster who did not delight in the use of his pocket-knife, if no more convenient tool were at hand, to display his *constructive*, and we fear but too often his *destructive*, capabilities? We hope that the advice we can give and the knowledge we shall endeavour to impart to *our* apprentices, in " Every Boy's Workshop," will reclaim all mischievous fellows, and encourage all those who are of an ingenious and constructive turn of mind. Just reflect, if it be only for a moment, how gratifying it would be to have it said,—" Don't send for Chips, the carpenter : my son can do the job quite as well; he is a capital joiner." Besides this, there are so many useful articles you would be able to make for the cost price of the material, and allowing a slight percentage on the original price of your tools.

Good tools are necessarily expensive, nevertheless our apprentices must use none but the best; for in the end they are the cheapest. Always remember the old and true saying, "A good workman is known by his tools." A good workman may do a tolerable job with indifferent tools, but a beginner should never attempt to use any but first-class implements, or he will never become a first-class craftsman. If you use bad tools, and try to cast the blame of bad work on them, recollect that "A bad workman always complains of his tools." A really clever mechanic cherishes his reputation far too highly to allow his tools to lapse into an inefficient condition; therefore, next to his character, the honest workman prides himself, and justly so, on the superior quality of his tools.

We are well aware that our apprentices cannot all afford to purchase good tools, to the extent they will require them, at a moment's notice; and, indeed, it is questionable whether it would be advantageous for them to do so at first under any circumstances, as increased confidence will be acquired by making a few tools serve for all purposes to which they can effectively be applied.

Many people imagine that when they have not a good set of carpenter's tools, the best plan is to purchase a box of so-called "Tools." Beware how you do this. Never buy a *box of tools*. A joiner's tool-chest, if bought of a respectable manufacturer, may be all right; but we do not advocate the practice.

Purchase, or, if you like, make a tool-chest, and furnish it with the best tools, carefully selected from the manufacturer's stock. A young carpenter will do well to get some friend who has the requisite experience to examine the tools before purchasing. We will quote the average prices of the best tools required for "Our Workshop;" our apprentices will then be able to judge of the qualities and prices offered by the makers with whom they may be obliged to deal.

Some little misconception exists respecting the terms, *carpenter, joiner,* and *cabinet-maker.* Strictly speaking, a carpenter is the artisan whose duty it is to lay down floors, build roofs, and make other substantial frame-work, of which many examples may be found in the building trade. A thorough carpenter is a very clever fellow; in fact, he is a scientific man,—an engineer in his way. Many of the most eminent builders were carpenters. Half the men who style themselves carpenters and joiners are really only the latter. A joiner begins where the carpenter leaves off. As soon as the roof, flooring, and other heavy work is finished, the joiner comes into the house, and fits the window-frames and sashes, doors, cupboards, shelves, &c., &c., which are essential to make a house habitable. All the fixtures being completed, our friends, the carpenter and joiner, leave the premises to the cabinet-maker, who supplies the furniture, &c., without which we should not feel much tempted to make a prolonged stay in the house, however cleverly his able predecessors had accomplished their allotted tasks.

CHAPTER I.

THE BENCH.

IT is our intention to notice many things, however trivial, that may in any way serve to enlighten our readers respecting the joiner's art. Many of the most extensive works are produced by the proper combination of several small, and, when taken singly, apparently unimportant devices.

Every one who has made an attempt at carpentry is aware that the object on which we wish to use our tools must be firmly fixed, in such a manner that we may apply our tools with convenience to the part to be wrought. The bench, of which fig. 1 is a representation, consists of a strong rough frame, surmounted by a stout top, formed of 2-inch board. The height of the bench should be about 2 feet 6 inches, but this must be regulated to some extent by the stature of the workman. The best way to determine the proper height for your bench is to place a plane on an ordinary table, and grasp it as though in the act of planing. If the back be straight, and the right elbow a *little* bent, the height is correct. You should feel that you have

Fig. 1.

entire command over the tool, which you cannot possess if the bench be much too high.

As we suppose that our shop is only about to be opened, it will probably be better to purchase a second-hand bench of some carpenter, which may be done for a few shillings. If you can afford to pay for a new bench, do not hesitate, but do so; because, next to good tools, a sound, steady bench is of great importance, as you will discover shortly, when we begin to use the plane. If the bench be about 5 feet long, and 2 feet 4 inches wide, it will be large enough. The upper surface of the bench should be smooth and true. Near the left-hand corner a square hole, or mortise, is cut, into which is fitted a block of hard wood, *S*, called the *stop*. The use of the stop is to check the wood that is to be planed, so that it may not be pushed forward when the plane-iron begins to cut. The stop is somewhat longer than the thickness of the top of the bench, so that it may be driven up with a mallet from below, to suit the thickness of the work to be planed; it can also be knocked down to clear thin works, so that the plane may pass over it without sticking.

It is frequently necessary to secure one piece of wood temporarily on another, when using the chisel. For this purpose, a peculiarly-shaped piece of wrought-iron, *h*, termed a *holdfast*, is employed. The holdfast acts in a very simple manner. The part you see above the bench is merely bent round, the end being turned up into a foot to press on the work. The lower part is a straight round bar, which, by being set askew in a hole made in the top of the bench, draws itself tighter the harder we strike the head at n, and thus forcibly presses down the work to be held; if struck at h, the work is released.

The screw-chops, C, also shown separately below, are of great service for holding work which may require planing on the edge, such as a long board, &c., and also for many purposes we shall notice hereafter. The chops consist of a face-board, C, which should be made of some hard wood, that is not liable to warp; mahogany is very good. Common benches are fitted with chops made of pine, which is generally the material of which the bench is itself constructed. The face-board is made to advance to the edge of the bench, or to recede therefrom, by a strong wooden screw, P, which works in a wooden nut, fixed to the underside of the bench. The face-board is guided by a square rail, r, which is secured thereto, the other end sliding in a suitable mortise, under the bench. The screw is moved by a round wooden bar, which passes through the head, P, the bar being an easy fit, to enable us to draw it through the head on either side as may be required; it is kept in its place by a head at each end.

We have given a list of the principal tools, &c., that you will require, and also illustrations of the more important amongst them. The prices quoted will be found to agree very nearly with those of the first London houses. Tools can undoubtedly be bought for less than half the sum here stated, but the quality, if they be sold as new, will be very inferior. A good set of joiner's tools, if properly used and taken care of, will last and be serviceable for two average lifetimes.

All the edge-tools should be made of the best cast-steel, otherwise they will not remain sharp for even a short time. Shear-steel is very suitable for many purposes in which elasticity or toughness is required; but it cannot be advantageously employed for edge-tools. If the steel be too hard, the edge breaks away; if too soft, the tool quickly becomes blunt, owing to the edge turning up. There are few things more annoying to a workman than to be obliged to sharpen his chisels and planes much more frequently than would otherwise be necessary if the steel were good.

Carpentry and Joinery.

LIST OF TOOLS REQUIRED FOR "OUR WORKSHOP."

(Average Prices.)

	£	s.	d.
Small hand-saw	0	4	0
Sash and tenon-saw	0	5	0
Table and compass-saw	0	1	6
Axe	0	2	0
Jack-plane (double iron)	0	5	6
Smoothing-plane	0	4	0
Spokeshave	0	2	6
Cutting-gauge	0	1	0
Marking-gauge	0	1	0
Four firmer-chisels, $\frac{1}{4}$, $\frac{1}{2}$, $\frac{3}{4}$, 1-in.	0	3	6
Three mortise-chisels, $\frac{1}{4}$, $\frac{1}{2}$, $\frac{5}{8}$-in.	0	3	6
Three gouges $\frac{1}{2}$, $\frac{3}{4}$, $1\frac{1}{4}$-in.	0	3	0
Gimlets and bradawls	0	1	0
Joiner's hammer	0	2	0
Mallet	0	3	0
Screwdriver	0	2	0
Brace (36 black bits)	1	10	0
Pincers	0	1	0
Compasses	0	1	0
Square	0	3	0
Bevil	0	3	0
Rule	0	2	0
Grindstone	1	0	0
Oilstone	0	4	0
Oil can	0	1	0
Gluepot	0	2	6
	£5	12	0

Depend upon it, there is no policy more short-sighted than to sacrifice quality for cheapness. Those who are unable to afford the stock-in-trade we have proposed, must content themselves with purchasing a tool occasionally. A good deal of work may be done with a hand-saw, tenon-saw, jack-plane, a firmer-chisel, one gouge, marking-gauge, one gimlet, one bradawl, screwdriver, hammer, mallet, square, rule, oil-stone, oil-can, and glue-pot, costing about thirty-six shillings.

The other tools may very well be postponed until your capital will admit of the investment.

CHAPTER II.

HOW TO USE THE TOOLS.

CARPENTRY, like every other important art, demands much attentive practice, before even a moderate degree of proficiency can be acquired. Any one accustomed to mechanical manipulation can tell whether a man is a skilled or an indifferent workman, by noticing the way in which he handles his tools. A novice thinks, when he sees an expert carpenter at work, that it requires no great skill to saw, to plane, or to bore a hole; and that any one can drive a nail or put in a screw. What we say is, let our tyro try his hand at any of these apparently easy jobs. He will very soon ask why the saw won't cut straight, or the plane make the wood flat; why, in boring the hole, the wood always splits, the nails goes askew, and the screw won't hold; and, we may add, our young friend discovers that carpentry is not so soon mastered as he thought.

The saw being the first tool the carpenter must use to reduce his materials to the rough dimensions, we will consider it first. On examination it will be observed that the steel or blade of the saw is thinner on the back than on the toothed edge. The object of this reduction in the thickness is to enable the saw to move with greater freedom in the *kerf*, as the saw-cut is called. If the blade were of the same substance from the front to the back edge, we should be unable to drive the saw after it had fairly entered on its work, owing to the great side friction. Another provision for still further facilitating the movements of the saw is called the *set* of the teeth. By this is meant the alternate side inclination of the teeth. By bending the teeth alternately to the right and left, they act more on the sides of the kerf, and make it wider than the thickness of the blade, which, being at liberty, can move freely. Setting a saw is a nice operation, and it requires much practice to do well. An amateur should never attempt to set or rather re-set his saws, as he will in all probability spoil them. If a saw be set more on one side than on the other, it will generally go astray on that side, and will require considerable attention to keep it to the line. The saw, if bought of a good manufacturer, will in all probability work quite satisfactorily; but we consider it necessary to point out the difficulties which may arise, and advise our pupils as to the best course to be pursued.

Suppose we require to make a rough box or any similar object, which is formed by fastening several boards together. The saw (fig. 2) must necessarily be used to reduce the wood to the right size, before we can be said to have commenced our task. The plank to be sawn is generally placed across two low stools or trestles about twenty inches in height. We must then mark a chalk or pencil line to indicate the path of the saw. If the plank be too wide for our

Fig. 2.—Hand-saw.

purpose, the saw must be employed in the direction of the grain, or in the lengthway of the plank. The plank must overhang one of the trestles a few inches, and the saw, which is to be held in the right hand, can then be advantageously applied. You must stand a little behind the trestle which supports the overhanging end of the plank, and place your right knee on the plank to keep it steady. The first incision should be made with the small end of the saw, the strokes being short and quick. As the saw advances, the stroke may be increased, until almost the entire serrated edge comes into action. The overhanging end of the wood must be supported by the left hand, the fingers being below, the thumb alone resting on the upper side. The left hand is also employed to draw the plank forward when the saw approaches the trestle. The labour of sawing may be considerably diminished by occasionally greasing the blade with a tallow candle end, or the tallow may be smeared on a piece of leather, and so be more conveniently applied. Sawing with the grain is called *ripping*, and the tool employed for this purpose is called a *rip-saw*, the teeth of which are large and of a triangular shape. When you have ripped a sufficiently long piece of "stuff" to form the four sides of the box, supposing the plank to be long enough, the saw can be applied across the grain at right angles to the first kerf, the plank being held only by the left hand behind the new kerf. Just before the second kerf meets the first, the wood about to be severed must be supported by the left hand, and the saw must be used gently to avoid breaking a piece of the wood away when the kerfs meet. If care be not observed, a large piece or splinter will tear from either side, and perhaps unfit the wood for the purpose for which it was intended.

Carpentry and Joinery. 17

If the box is only to be made in the "rough,"—that is, not planed, and simply nailed together,—you must saw the stuff as straight as possible, otherwise it will indeed be a rough job. If the plane is to be used, the wood must be sawn across for the sides after it has been planed, otherwise it will be more difficult to make the thickness uniform.

Sawing forms so important a part of the carpenter's work, that we may surely be excused if we dwell a little longer on the management of this tool. Our readers will do well if they practise sawing as extensively as their limited opportunities will admit.

If the plank be thick and the length to be sawn considerable, the work should be frequently turned over to equalize any irregularity that may arise from unskilful guidance of the saw. The work must therefore be marked out on both sides, care being taken to make the lines coincide with each other exactly, or they will be worse than useless.

While sawing, the eye must be vigilant, and should appreciate the slightest departure from the line. The eye must be directed only so much to the right or left of the edge of the blade, that the line may be seen on either side on the slightest movement of the head to the right or left. If the eye be suffered to wander, so that the line is seen entirely—say on the right —the hand will involuntarily force the saw in that direction, and the blade will pursue an erratic course. If the saw has not departed much from its proper course, it may be restored to the line by twisting the handle a little in the opposite direction to that which the saw has taken. We are enabled to do this the more readily owing to the set of the teeth, which has made the kerf a little wider than the blade, and the reduction in the thickness of the blade towards the back edge affords additional freedom. Care, however, must be observed in this correctional or steering process, otherwise the saw will be made to err as much in the opposite direction, and the blade may be jammed fast in the kerf.

The toothed edge of the saw should be held nearly vertically in the thrust, or cutting strokes. If it be allowed to become much inclined to the work, the depth to be sawn is practically increased, and the labour proportionally augmented. When the wood is very hard or thick, the saw must be grasped with both hands; the difficulty of directing its course is then, however, much increased. Sometimes the wood to be sawn is too short to be conveniently held on the trestle. When this is the case, it must be fixed either on the bench or in the screw chops.

If we required to saw a short piece of board, about ten or twelve inches in length, we should fix it in an upright position in the chops, and hold the upper end of the wood with the left hand, and drive the saw with the right. This is a favourite position with many workmen, who prefer the erect to the stooping attitude. It is of great importance to become habituated to certain defined positions when at work; for if the body be inclined at one time and erect at another, the character of the work remaining unchanged, no accuracy can be expected, as the action of the tools is greatly influenced by the posture of the workman. If the work be fixed on the bench so that the part to be sawn overhangs a few inches, the saw must be held with both hands, and allowed to hang down in front of the operator, the toothed edge being from him and towards the work. As the tool cuts, the carpenter advances, still maintaining the saw in its pendent position. Careful practice is the only way in which you can attain skill, not only in mechanical operations, but in everything, however trivial it may be, that you undertake.

Our pupils should take every opportunity of watching practical men at work, and should never suffer a silly, false pride to hinder them from asking for information, which, if properly solicited, will never be withheld. A clever, intelligent workman feels a proper pride in the art he professes, and is really gratified when a young fellow asks him to solve the difficulties which all amateurs are certain to experience in their undertakings.

For the present we must lay aside the saw, and examine the plane, which is the tool by which the smooth, finished appearance is imparted to all carpentry and joinery works.

The plane consists of a long, narrow piece of

Fig. 3.—Jack-plane.

hard wood, made as true and smooth in every direction as possible.

Fig. 3 will give you a general idea of the *Jack-plane*, which is used for reducing the rough wood to a uniform surface. The iron, as the cutting blade is called, is in shape very similar

Fig. 4.—Firmer-chisel.

to a firmer-chisel (fig. 4). A wedge-shaped

opening is made through the wood or stock of the plane, in which the iron is inserted. The narrow end of the wedge-shaped opening is at the bottom of the sole or stock, through which the sharp edge of the iron slightly projects.

As it is not only important, but absolutely necessary, that the workman should understand the construction of the tools he uses, we must request our pupils attentively to examine the several views of the plane we are about to consider.

Fig. 5 is a section taken through the length of the stock, dividing it in the middle or centre

Fig. 5.

of its width. The iron, *a b*, is clearly seen; also the wedge, *w*, by which the iron is firmly fixed in the inclined position. The solid wood behind the iron, on which it rests, is called the *bed*. The narrow opening at *a* is the *mouth*, and the inclined wall at *a c* is called the *wear*. The angle of the wear should not be great, otherwise the wearing away of the sole of the plane will tend to enlarge the mouth; at the same time the angle must not be too slight, or the plane will *choke;* that is, the shavings will stick fast, and prevent the tool working. The second inclined wall, *c d,* is termed the *front,* the angle of which is unimportant.

The mouth is generally about one-third of the length of the plane from the front end, not only

Fig. 6.—Smoothing-plane.

in the long, but also in the smoothing-planes. The dotted lines, *e f* (fig. 5), show where the stock would stop in a smoothing-plane, in which the iron is similar. Fig. 6 is a general representation of a smoothing-plane. The wedge for fixing the iron is shown in two views in fig. 7.

Fig. 7.

The handle, or toat, *t,* by which the plane is driven forward, is simply in the form of a horn, as in figs. 3 and 5, for these and panel-planes;

but longer planes have handles, fixed in the same relation to the iron, but in shape they much resemble the handle of a hand-saw.

Most of the surfacing-planes are fitted with

Fig. 8.

"double irons." The irons are shown in section to a larger scale in fig. 8. The lower iron, *a a*, is the cutter, while the upper, or *break*-iron, *b b*,

Fig. 9.

only bends the shavings out of the way of the edge of the iron proper, and directs them up the "wear." The end, *b*, of the break-iron, is formed with a large curve, and the edge which rests on the cutter is made only moderately sharp, as it is

Fig. 10.

not required to cut. The two irons are fastened together by the screw, *s*, which is "tapped" into the boss, *t*, formed on the break-iron, which is shown separately in fig. 10. The cutter is seen disconnected from the break-iron in fig. 9. The long slot, m, enables us to adjust the irons longitudinally, and also, to a slight extent, sideways. The round hole, h, is a little larger than the head of the screw, s, to permit the latter to pass through when we wish to separate the irons, which is accomplished by unslacking the screw about one turn, and sliding the break-iron back towards the hole, h. The break-iron of the jack-plane is generally fixed, so that its edge is one-sixteenth or one-fifteenth of an inch behind the edge of the cutter. If the break-iron be set back, say one-eighth of an inch, it will not bend the shavings sufficiently, and the planing will very probably be rough. The nearer the edges of the irons are to each other, within certain limits, the smoother will be the work produced, but the labour of driving the plane will be much increased. The edges of the irons are set farther apart in the jack and similar planes than in the smoothing-planes, as the surface of the work is not finished until a more advanced stage.

Planes having single irons are much less laborious to handle, but the work executed by them is neither so smooth nor so truthful as that of the double-ironed description. The shavings escape in long curls or ribands from a single iron, and the surface of the work is left somewhat rough. It is a good plan to remove the first exterior and dirt from a plank with a single-ironed plane, after which the jack and smoothing-planes will work pleasantly, and retain their edges for a longer time.

The inclination or angle at which the iron is fixed in the stock is called the "pitch." The pitch is regulated according to the nature of the wood on which the plane is to be used. If the workman be using material of a hard and close nature, the iron must have much less inclination than would be correct for soft woods, such as deal or pine. The pitch cannot be varied in ordinary planes, therefore two or more planes, each having a different pitch, must be provided, if the work demands much change in the character of the wood.

The lowest, or *common pitch*, for surfacing-planes for soft woods, like pine or deal, is forty-five degrees from the horizontal line of the sole; *York pitch*, or fifty degrees, is suitable for mahogany, rosewood, &c.; *middle pitch*, or fifty-five degrees, is the general angle for irons of moulding-planes for soft woods, and is also correct for smoothing-planes for hard materials; *half-pitch*, or sixty degrees, for moulding-planes for mahogany, rosewood, and other woods which are liable to "tear up." Still harder substances, such as boxwood, ivory, &c., require planes in which the pitch entirely disappears, the iron being fixed vertically. In some instances the pitch is reversed by inclining the iron a little in the opposite direction. Both these planes are properly scrapers, and they only remove the material in the shape of dust.

Having considered the general construction of the bench-planes, we will now offer a few suggestions respecting their management.

Before setting to work, the irons must be sharpened and adjusted. The iron is disengaged from the stock by striking the latter on the back end behind the "toat;" the same may also be effected by a moderate blow on the upper surface near the front end. The hammer should never be used with violence, as two or three light taps will liberate the iron and not bruise the stock. The wedge may also be loosened by tapping it on either side alternately, and, when sufficiently slack, it can be withdrawn by the fingers.

The screw which secures the break-iron to the cutter must be turned back about one revolution by the aid of a large screwdriver, the break-iron can then be slipped back till the head of the screw enters the hole, h (fig. 9), in the cutter, when the irons can be separated.

If the iron be very blunt, it must first be ground and then set on the oilstone or hone. The grindstone (fig. 11, page 27) should be of a fine and moderately quick cutting description. Probably the "bilstone" is the best quality for amateur purposes. It is important that the stone should run true, and the circumference to which the tools are applied must be either quite flat or a little rounded, and should never be suffered to become hollow, or lower at the centre than at the edges. The iron must be firmly held by

Fig. 11.— Grindstone.

both hands, and applied to the stone at an angle of about twenty-five degrees. The stone should revolve towards the edge, to avoid forming a "wire edge," which is ragged and saw-like, and not at all sharp. The iron must be held at one constant angle, for if it be raised higher at one time than at another, the chamfer or bevil, a, will not be ground to a uniform face, but will either be rounding or in a series of flats. Though the iron must be held rigidly with respect to the chamfer, yet it is necessary to move it backwards and forwards across the face of the stone, to preserve the latter from unequal wear, and this management is also necessary to enable us to make the edge of the iron straight. If the stone were a little hollow on the face, the corners of iron would be ground away, leaving the middle too prominent. On the other hand, if the stone were rounding or highest at the middle, the iron

Fig. 12.

would, if kept stationary, be ground away at the centre, and not at the corners.

Grinding plane-irons and firmer-chisels is a nice operation, and requires much practice to do properly. It is generally found difficult to restore the iron to the stone exactly at the same angle after it has been temporarily withdrawn for inspection. The wrists ought to be kept rigidly fixed, and the arms should be held closely to the sides, to impart as much firmness as possible to the hands. If the iron be weakly held, it will be impossible to grind it to a uniform face, as the motion of the stone exerts a powerful influence in changing its position.

The iron being satisfactorily ground on the chamfer, it must now be set on the oilstone to make its edge smooth and keen. It must be stated that the flat side of the iron should never

Fig. 13.

be applied to the grindstone, as any slight burr can be much better removed by the oilstone.

Fig. 12 shows the position in which the iron should be applied to the oilstone. The iron is first grasped in the right hand, the fingers being placed on the surface and the thumb turned underneath, as in fig. 13. The fingers of the left hand must now be lapped over those of the right, and the thumb must also be placed below to support the iron. Some people place all, excepting the fore-finger, below the iron, and lap the left thumb over the right. Either of these methods is good.

The oilstone, like the grindstone, requires uniform wear to keep it in good order.

Next to the "Turkey oilstone," the "Charnley Forest" is esteemed by joiners and others as the best for giving a fine edge to various tools. The stone should be fixed in a wooden case, provided with a cover to exclude the dust when it is not in use. Sperm oil is the best for sharpening purposes; but neatsfoot is cheaper, and may be considered as a fair substitute, being devoid of unpleasant smell, and not liable to thicken.

The plane-iron should be held at a constant angle of about thirty-five degrees, and must be kept square across the face of the stone. If the stone be narrower than the iron, the latter must be worked from side to side, to reduce the corners uniformly with the middle. If the iron be set askew, so that one corner moves in advance of the other, the foremost corner will be ground away too rapidly, and the edge of the iron will no longer be square to the sides. When the edge is required to be slightly rounded, as for rough work, a light roll must be given to the blade edgeways, but a decided, though small chamfer, should be imparted to the irons of smoothing-planes, and as distinct in its formation as the larger one made by the grindstone. Much pressure should be avoided, as the edge is liable to bend over, and become what is called "wire edge." The flat side of the iron must now be laid *quite flat* on the stone, and gently rubbed a few times to remove any "wire edge" which may have formed. Under any circumstances, this finishing process is advantageous.

If the iron be held too upright, the edge is more quickly produced, but it will remain sharp for a much shorter time than if it had been set at a lower inclination. It is obvious that if the iron were sharpened at an angle of forty-five degrees, which is the pitch at which it is fixed in the stock, the chamfer formed by the oilstone would rest on the work, and consequently would act only as a burnisher. On the other hand, if the angle be very acute, the edge will be too thin to be durable; therefore the angle of thirty-five degrees already stated appears as favourable as any.

The irons of the jack and other long planes are ground with a large curve or arc, to make the centre part of the blade slightly in advance of the corners. This method has the effect of reducing the labour which would otherwise be required to urge the plane forward. The irons of smoothing-planes, though made as flat and straight as possible on the edge, are, nevertheless, slightly rounded at the corners, to prevent their leaving marks on the work.

The workman judges of the condition of the cutter after setting it on the oilstone, partly by the eye and partly by sense of touch. The edge may look regular and sharp, yet it may not be sufficiently keen to penetrate the hardened skin of the hand when gently drawn across it, which is the almost universal test to which the cutter is applied before reinserting it in the stock.

The cutter being satisfactorily set, the break-iron must be attached. If the plane is to be used for coarse work, like removing the rough outside of a board, &c., the edge of the break-iron may be fixed about one-sixteenth of an inch from the edge of the cutter. The sides of the break-iron should be parallel with those of the cutter, and the corners of the latter must be equidistant from the edge of the break-iron. If it be found that one corner of the cutter is nearer the break-iron than the other, the edge of the cutter has not been ground and set square to its sides. If the discrepancy be considerable, the cutter must be reground to rectify the error. If the break-iron be set back one-sixteenth of an inch from the edge of the cutter at the centre, and one corner of the cutter stands below the edge of the break-iron, regrinding is inevitable.

Supposing the irons to be true to each other,

they may now be fixed in the stock. The cutter must be laid on the "bed," and be passed down until the edge is level with the sole of the stock. The wedge is next put in, and gently tapped to prevent the irons falling out. The plane must then be held so that the upper corner of the back end may rest on the bench, while the front end is supported by the right hand. The eye can now be directed along the sole, to appreciate the quantity the iron is made to project, by tapping it lightly with the hammer, which is held in the left hand. When the edge appears slightly prominent, the wedge must be knocked in a little tighter, but violence should be carefully avoided. The iron should at all times be slenderly held, otherwise the stock will be distorted. If in driving the wedge forward the iron should also advance, it may be withdrawn by striking a moderate blow on the upper surface of the stock near the front end, and this without altering the position of the plane. Should one corner of the edge project more than the other, the iron and wedge must be slackened by a blow on the stock; the iron can then be set square by a few taps on the opposite corner at its upper end. By a few well-directed blows of the hammer the edge may be satisfactorily adjusted, but some practice is required to regulate the iron so nicely by eye, that the plane will act properly without subsequent correction. It may perhaps be found on trial that the iron does not project sufficiently to cut; a light tap on the top of the iron will probably set this right. Perhaps the iron stands forward too much, and either entirely opposes the action of the plane, or renders the cut coarse and rough; this may be rectified by one or two light blows, either on the upper surface of the stock near the front end, or on the back extremity.

These instructions equally apply to the smoothing-plane. This latter being required to produce as smooth a surface as possible, the break-iron is fixed much more closely to the edge of the cutter, the fortieth or fiftieth of an inch being the common measure.

The planes being in good order, the wood to be planed must be laid on the bench, the stop, S, fig. 1, being adjusted so as to stand about one-eighth of an inch below the general level of the plank. If two opposite corners of the plank be higher than the other parts, the board is "in winding;" and if the edges or the middle be the most prominent, it is said to be "cast." If the plank be thin, it may be somewhat straightened by holding one end firmly on the bench, and twisting the other in the opposite direction to that in which it is distorted. If the wood be too hard or thick to admit of this treatment, the prominences must be removed by the plane.

Carpentry and Joinery.

The proper way to hold the jack and similar planes is shown in fig. 14. The toat or handle is firmly grasped by the right hand, while the left is placed about half-way between the front end of the plane and the mouth. The thumb of the left hand is towards the workman, and all the fingers are placed on the off-side of the tool. The principal part of the force necessary to urge the plane forward is transmitted by the right hand

Fig. 14.

through the handle or toat, the left hand acting more as a guide, and to keep the front of the plane down to its work, than as a motor, though it does undoubtedly assist in that way to some extent.

If the plank be either "cast" or "in winding," the prominent parts must first be cropped off by running the jack-plane over them respectively, until the plank is made roughly level. The plane must then be driven from one end of the board to the other, if its length be under four feet; at all events, the shavings should be at least two feet six inches or three feet in length, to insure the accurate working of the tool. The plane requires to be kept firmly down to its work, which is done more by allowing the weight of the body to rest on it through the arms, than by any direct muscular effort. If the plane be making a good continuous shaving, the workman should endeavour, by moving the plane with a steady and uninterrupted motion, to carry it to the end of the work. This after a little practice is not difficult to achieve, for if the plane be in good order, and the "stuff" is tolerably straight, the workman after starting the cut can walk from one end of the work to the other, and keep the plane moving at the same uniform rate. It is not unfrequently found that the wood planes more smoothly from one end than from the other; it is therefore desirable to reverse the plank end for end if the grain "tears up," notwithstanding the use of a finely-set iron.

On the return stroke, the plane should not only be entirely relieved of all downward pressure, but the back end or heel should be slightly raised to prevent useless friction on the sole. When planing short pieces, the plane is generally lifted some little distance off the work.

When the rough exterior is removed and the plank has been made tolerably flat, the jack-plane should be laid aside for the trying-plane. If our readers do not possess this tool, which is similar in character, only considerably longer, than the jack-plane, they must reset their jack-plane and fix the break-iron very close to the edge of the cutter, and adjust this latter with a very fine cut. After a few strokes have been made over the general surface of the plank, the work should be tested with a *straight-edge,* which is simply a thin bar of hard wood (mahogany or metal), which has been very carefully made, so as to insure an edge as accurately straight as possible. If the work be lower in the middle than at the ends, the straight-edge will only rest on the ends and not touch in the middle. This want of truth in the work is readily detected by the line of light which is seen between the edge of the straight-edge and the work, where the latter is "hollow." The curative treatment is obvious; we must lower the ends of the plank by planing a little off them, and so reduce them to a level with the lowest part.

If the work be highest at the middle, the straight-edge will rock as on a centre, owing to the ends being unsupported. If the discrepancy be so slight as to occasion neither a decided rocking nor to show a line of light, the seat of error may be discovered by holding the straight-edge at the centre between the forefinger and thumb, and twisting or rotating it slowly backwards and forwards for a short distance. If the highest part of the work be immediately under the centre of the straight-edge, it will be plainly felt at that point, and the ends will move quite freely; but if the straight-edge rests on two or more points on either side of the centre, the fact is made apparent by the increased resistance offered to its movements.

In the preparatory stage, before the work has become sufficiently true to require the severer test of the straight-edge, its approach towards accuracy is tried by placing the edge of the plane obliquely across it in the manner of a straight-edge. The workman also raises one end of the work to the level of his eye and glances along it, or if the work be too large to be conveniently lifted, he stoops to attain the same relative position, and in this way at once discovers the undulations which are to be rectified.

If the work is to be planed on both sides it should now be " gauged to thickness," and turned over, as the second side must be made true before the final finish is put on the first. It will be almost invariably found that the board will cast a little on the removal of the rough outside: it would therefore be a waste of labour to complete one side before touching the other; in fact, the endeavour should always be to carry on the work so that the opposite parts may balance each other as nearly as possible, and thereby avoid distortion.

The two sides or "surfaces" of the board being now true and flat, the edges must next be

Fig. 15.

"shot" or planed. To do this conveniently the board should be fixed in the screw-chops of the bench (C, fig. 1). Fig. 15 illustrates the manner of fixing the wood and handling the plane. The front end only of the plank can be held in the chops, the other extremity is therefore supported by a small iron bolt, which is slipped into one of a series of holes made for that purpose in some convenient part of the frame of the bench. It will be seen that in "shooting" an edge, the left hand is differently applied to the front end of the plane to what it is when surfacing. The thumb is allowed to rest on the top of the plane, and the fingers are bent under the sole to support it, the narrow edge of the board not affording sufficient base to keep the plane steady. The truth of the edge can be tested longitudinally by looking along it, and also by trying it with the straight-edge. The edge not only requires to be straight in the direction of its length, but it must also be made *square* to the sides.

Fig. 16.—The Square.

The square (fig. 16) is the tool by which the truth of all right-angled surfaces is ascertained. The joiner's square consists of a steel blade, which is made quite straight on the edges, which also require to be perfectly parallel to each other. This blade is firmly fixed exactly at right angles in a stock formed of hard wood, which is faced with brass on the inner edge to

Carpentry and Joinery. 41

increase its durability. The inner edge of the stock must be firmly held against the flat surface of the board, taking care that it rests fairly ; the square must then be gradually lowered till the edge of the blade comes in contact with the edge of the board. If the edge be square to the sides, the blade of the square will touch throughout the thickness of the board, but if the work be untrue, the blade of the square will rest on the highest point, which must be reduced till the square bears fairly. The square must be applied at intervals of a few inches throughout the length of the plank, and frequently during the progress of the work.

Fig. 17.—Rule.

When the edge has been made true, both in the longitudinal and cross directions, the board must be removed from the chops and laid flat on the bench. The finished width of the board is now to be marked. If the plank be more than six inches wide, the rule (fig. 17) will be the proper means to employ. Suppose the plank is required to be six inches wide throughout its length or parallel, the width can be measured and marked at each end on the surface; a straight-edge must then be adjusted to the marks and a line ruled. If the work to be marked is only two or three inches wide, the *marking-gauge* (fig. 18) is used. This tool is made of hard wood, and consists simply of a stem

Fig. 18.—Marking-gauge.

furnished with a closely-fitting block, which is capable of sliding stiffly along it, and of being fixed in any desired position, either by a wedge or a set screw. Near one end of the stem a flat steel point or scriber is inserted, for marking or scoring a line on the work. The point should not project more than one thirty-second part of an inch, or it will make a deep unsightly mark.

To adjust the gauge it is only necessary to slacken the wedge or screw which fixes the movable block or head, and to hold the latter in the hand and strike either end of the stem against the bench, or tap it with the hammer. If the distance from the point of the scriber to the face of the head be two inches, and we wish to gauge a line, say two inches and a half, or any greater distance within the range of the gauge,

Fig. 19.

we must strike the opposite end of the stem to that in which the scriber is fixed ; and the reverse, if we desire it, to decrease the space between the head and the point.

The correct way of holding the marking-gauge is shown in fig. 19. The work, if light, is supported in an inclined position by the left hand, and the gauge is applied by the right. It is necessary to keep the head of the gauge firmly against the edge of the work to which it is wished to make the line parallel, otherwise any crookedness in the grain of the wood will be liable to send the gauge askew.

We have, though unavoidably, wandered from the operation we had in hand, viz., the planing of a board, to which we at once hasten to return.

Fig. 20.

Both edges of the plank are now supposed to be true and parallel to each other; it is therefore only necessary to finish the surfaces with the smoothing-plane to complete our first attempt at carpentry. Fig. 20 represents the manner of holding the *smoothing*-plane. The right hand is placed behind the wedge, so that the thumb shall press against one side of the stock, and all the fingers on the other. The left hand is clasped round the front end of the plane, and the thumb rests on the upper surface. The workman has complete control over the plane, and if the grain of the wood be short and cross, or hard, knotty, or tough, he imparts a "side-long" sweep to the tool, which somewhat facilitates its action as a smoother by enabling it to attack the grain as favourably as possible. If the wood be clean and of uniform hardness, the course of the plane should be quite straight, and the strokes of moderate length. At the termination of every stroke the plane is entirely lifted off the work, and is reapplied at any point, where, either from the indication of the straight-edge or the appearance of the work, it may be deemed requisite by the carpenter.

If the thin "stuff" which we have "planed up" be intended for forming the "carcase" of a box or any similar piece of rectangular work, the sides must now be marked out and cut off. The plank is suffered to lie flat on the bench, and the square is applied, so that the stock may rest fairly against one of the edges which has been carefully planed. The square must be adjusted, so that the *outer* edge of the blade may be *within* the *lowest* part of the end of the plank, which is next the "stop" of the bench. A pencil line is now to be marked, taking care that it be perfectly square to the edges of the plank. The board must next be removed and fixed in the chops of the bench, so that the end just marked may stand a little above them. The end is supposed to have been sawn tolerably square to the edges, when the wood was "roughed out;" but if, owing to bad workmanship, the end is much out of truth with the line marked from the square, the saw must be employed to remove the greater part of the material, previously to applying the plane. The smoothing-plane must be very finely set, otherwise it will "tear up" the fibre of the wood, which is exceedingly fragile in the cross direction of the grain. The plane must be used cautiously when shooting the ends, to avoid the "*spalling off*," that is, breaking away the fibre as a splinter on the front edge towards which the plane is moving. The tendency to "spall off" may be lessened by holding the plane somewhat obliquely, to enable the iron to attack the fibre in the cross direction, and by *running off* the stroke by lifting the plane from the work just before the extreme corner is reached.

The result of this treatment will be to leave the far corner too high, but this can be rectified by turning the board and bringing the *front* edge towards the workman. The plane is again used as before, till the high corner is reduced to the proper level. The square must now be applied from the edge, to discover if the end be truly at right angles to it, and also from the surface, to test the accuracy in the direction of the thickness. Before using the square, any roughness on the edges of the work must be removed, otherwise the square will fail to indicate its actual condition, and will lead the workman astray.

If the longitudinal edges of the work be strictly parallel to each other, the end of the work will be square, or at right angles to both of them. By applying the square to the edges respectively any discrepancy which may exist will be made apparent.

Sometimes the square is untrue. If the blade be badly fitted or ill-secured in the stock it is liable to shift, and occasion much trouble. The truth of the square may easily be tested by applying the stock to the edge of a board, which has been carefully "shot," and drawing a line against the outer and inner edges of the blade. The square must then be turned over, and if the edges still agree with the lines it is true. It may also be tested by another square which is known to be accurate.

The length of one side of the box is now measured off from the end which has just been completed, and a line is squared across. The saw must be kept outside this line, which is to be approached only by the plane. The end of the plank is again squared and planed up, and and so on successively until the four sides are cut off. The opposite end of each of the sides must then be planed, after which the carcase may be nailed or glued together. The various methods of uniting works will be considered hereafter.

If the work be thin, the edges are not sufficiently wide to afford a steady base for the sole

Fig. 21.

of the plane, consequently the difficulty of "shooting the edge true" is materially increased. The *shooting-board* is a valuable auxiliary when the work to be planed is long and thin. Fig. 21 is an end, and fig. 22 a perspective view of a shooting-board, suitable for the longitudinal edges of work. It consists of a stout plank, about four feet long and sixteen inches wide. To the upper side of this piece, which is called the *bed*, and which must be quite true, is secured a strip, C D, of the same length, and about two-thirds of the width of the bed. A stop, s, is fixed at the end of the strip, to keep the work steady. It is important that the strip on which the work, w w, is laid be quite flat, and square to the upper side of the bed, A B, to which it is permanently fixed by screws.

If the bed and strip of the shooting-board be true, and the side of the plane, which rests and slides on the bed, be strictly at right angles to

Fig. 22.

the sole, the edges of the work will be made accurately square to its sides. The work must be tested with the square, and if the edges be not at right angles, the defect is probably occasioned by the "iron," which may not be square in the stock; a few taps on the corner of the iron will rectify the discrepancy.

Fig. 23 shows the work, w, placed at right angles to the course of the plane, to enable us to finish the end. It is important to have the end,

Fig. 23.

F, of the stop truly at right angles to the edge of the strip, against which the sole of the plane runs. The strip should be made as wide as possible, to afford room for a broad stop, which

Fig. 24.

is of much assistance in keeping the work square while it is being planed.

Carpentry and Joinery. 51

The edge of work is sometimes beveled, instead of at right angles, to the sides. When this is to be done, the shooting-board must be modified, as in figs. 24 and 25. The bed, B, has a rebate planed along one of its edges, R, which fits a groove formed in the side of the board, T, the upper edge of which is beveled to the angle we desire to impart to the work, generally forty-five degrees.

Fig. 25.

If we require the end of the work to form any other than right angles with the edges, a separate block, I (fig. 26), of the correct angle, must be temporarily attached to the shooting-board, which is similar in every respect to the one represented in fig. 23. The loose blocks are usually made to an angle of forty-five degrees, which is very frequently employed in joinery works.

Fig. 26.

The stop of the shooting-board acts beneficially in checking the tendency to *spall off*, to which the work is so liable when planed across the grain. If the work be kept firmly against the stop, the wood, which otherwise might spall off, is well supported.

The use of the hand-saw and the plane seemed to call for special notice, but it is unnecessary to consider the several other tools employed by the carpenter and joiner, until we require them for our work.

CHAPTER III.

REMARKS ON THE SEASONING AND CHOICE OF THE WOODS.

IT is impossible to construct sound and durable work, if the material employed be green or unseasoned: the firmest joints that can be made will part, and the entire fabric become distorted and worthless. The practical carpenter is well aware of this, and if he be wise and value his reputation, he will spare no pains to insure the complete seasoning of his timber.

The winter is the usual season for felling timber, at which time the wood is less copiously charged with sap, owing to the circulation being almost entirely checked by the cold. After the trunk is cut down, it is allowed to remain untouched for a few months, but it should be sheltered from the direct influence of the sun, otherwise the exposed parts are liable to become *shaken* or cracked. The next stage in the seasoning commences after the trunk is sawn into planks, which, being comparatively thin, and presenting two sides to the atmosphere, materially hasten the process. While in the entire form, the evaporation of moisture from the wood could only proceed slowly, consequently the planks still contain much sap.

The planks are now formed into a stack, which must be raised a few feet from the ground, and especial care must be taken to keep the wood from actual contact, by inserting narrow strips between the ends of the planks, and also at distances of about eight feet apart. By this arrangement a free circulation of air is insured, and the seasoning is favourably and expeditiously accomplished.

Even timber in the stack is not entirely free from the ravages of the "shake," which will attack the ends of the planks; and the uppermost layer, which serves as a roof to the remainder, is frequently almost destroyed by the changes from wet to dry.

Thin planks, if judiciously stacked, will generally season in about eighteen months, but thick pieces require a much longer exposure. The timber must not be employed for works of importance immediately on its removal from the stack. The carpenter places several planks in racks, which retain them in a vertical position near his shop, and shortly before "working the stuff" he removes it inside the house to insure its complete seasoning.

If the seasoning be carried forward too rapidly, or is forced by subjecting the material to the direct influence of the fire, it is deprived of its toughness and elasticity; or, as the carpenter would say, "the nature has been taken out of it." If the timber is to be durable, the seasoning must be gradual and complete.

Though the wood may have been thoroughly seasoned, it is impossible to guard against the effects of change of temperature, and the liability to reabsorb moisture, if placed in a damp situation. On again becoming dry, the plank will probably no longer retain its former shape, but be more or less twisted or "in winding," which is a peculiar spiral twist, running through it in the direction of its length, so that if the board were laid on the bench, it would rest on two cross corners, on which it would rock.

Straight-grained woods are not subjected to any considerable change in the lengthway of the grain, but a distortion, called "warping," is very prevalent in the soft, as well as in the hard, varieties in the cross directions. Thin boards are sometimes curved like a bow in their cross sections. The joiner restores them to their original condition by ranging them round the shop, with the convex sides towards the fire, which, by evaporating the moisture, will cause the fibres of the wood to contract, and so bring it to its proper shape. The wood must not be too long exposed to the fire, or the remedy will be as bad or worse than the disease, as the board will become *concave* on the side next to the heat, and *convex* on the other, thus reversing, instead of removing, the evil. This may be avoided by frequently changing the sides when the boards have become flat, in order *to air* them equally.

Sometimes, when the wood is too much distorted to yield to the last-mentioned treatment, the joiner warms it equally on both sides to lessen its rigidity, and bends it as straight as he can by his hands. If the stuff will not retain the required shape, it must be again warmed, and placed between two stout planks, which are drawn closely together by handscrews.

If the plank to be wrought be too thick to admit of correction by the means just described, the prominences must be removed by the plane. No considerable distortion is to be feared in the straight-grained woods, such as pine and mahogany, provided the seasoning has been properly conducted. The finely-figured woods, which chiefly owe their beauty to the great irregularity of the grain, would be very liable to twist and warp, if employed in the same way as the straight-grained description. The handsomely-marked woods are too costly to admit of their being used of sufficient thickness for the top of a table, the sides of a box, or any similar article. The wood is therefore cut into very thin slices, called *veneer*, which is glued on the plain wood of which the fabric is constructed.

The amateur should always keep a stock of well-seasoned wood in his shop, and should never use material which has lately been taken from the carpenter's rack.

When choosing his woods, the amateur must be careful to select "clean stuff," free from *knots*, *shakes*, and *doats*. "Doats" are black stains, occasioned by the confined sap which has not evaporated, owing to the planks having rested in contact during their seasoning in the stack.

Pine, also commonly called *Deal*, is very largely employed in house-carpentry and other works. It is very clean and straight in grain, of a light colour, and easily wrought. The colour is much influenced by the quantity of resinous matter or turpentine contained in its pores, which imparts either a red or yellow tinge to the wood, from which peculiarity has arisen the distinctive titles of red and yellow deals.

Spruce is of the same family, but of inferior quality. It is of a harder nature and whiter colour, and, owing to the knots with which it abounds, is seldom employed for any except the commonest purposes. These woods are natives of cold countries, where they thrive the best. Our largest supplies of this valuable timber are exported from Norway, Baltic Port, Memel, Riga, and Dantzic.

Oak is a very hard and durable wood, easily distinguishable by its yellowish-brown colour. The English oak is esteemed the best, and is very extensively employed for ship-building, carpentry, substantial framing, and other works requiring considerable strength. It is little affected by exposure to the weather, and is therefore much used for numerous outdoor works, for the spokes and naves of wheels, &c. Some kinds, having a red tinge, are inferior to the brown, and are used only for ornamental furniture.

Elm is a very useful wood, and exceedingly durable if employed in wet or damp situations. It is unrivalled for dock-works, rough pumps, water-works, piles for foundations, keels of vessels, boards of coffins, and many similar purposes. In drying, it shrinks and twists very much, and is inapplicable to works in which permanence of form is imperative. Elm is porous and cross-grained, but it is not liable to split, and bears the driving of nails better than any other timber.

The colour is a dull red-brown, and much darker than oak.

Ash is a tough and very flexible wood; it is not, however, suitable for building purposes. It is much used for the frames of machines, felloes of wheels, agricultural implements, hand-spikes, handles of hammers, and many similar works. For works subjected to sudden and severe strains, ash may be considered superior to any other timber, its elasticity being so perfect that it may be bent almost double without breaking.

Beech is not employed for building, but is excellent for piles in wet foundations and similar works. This wood is naturally hard and of a close, firm texture. It is extensively used for the frames of machines, furniture, stocks of planes, handles of tools, and lathe-chucks. When stained and polished it looks exceedingly well.

Birchwood is much esteemed by the turner. It is compact in the grain, of a darker colour, and more easily worked than beech. . Some pieces of this wood are as handsomely marked as Honduras mahogany, and, when polished, may be easily mistaken for it.

Mahogany.—Of this wood there are two varieties, viz., Spanish and Honduras. The former is in every respect superior to the latter, and is generally, owing to its great beauty, cut into veneers, which are glued on stout fabrics constructed of Honduras or Baywood, which, though not often finely figured, is exceedingly good for the inside works of furniture. It is of a reddish-brown colour, sometimes open and irregular in the grain, and the inferior kinds are filled with specks and short grey lines. Some few specimens are of a fine golden colour, with handsome veins and figures.

For furniture and other indoor works, mahogany is unrivalled. It shrinks less in drying than any other wood, is susceptible of a high polish, and is little liable to twist or warp, and holds the glue the best of all. Foundry patterns are often made of it, as it resists the moisture of the damp sand, which does not, therefore, adhere to it so readily as to a softer wood. Mahogany is also in much request amongst turners.

Rosewood is another valuable furniture wood. Its colour varies from light hazel to deep purple, or nearly black. Some specimens are as open in the grain as coarse mahogany, but the best qualities are cut into veneers; and even solid pieces are used for cabinet and upholstery works. The harder kinds may be very highly polished, but it seldom retains its lustre so long as mahogany.

"Mr. Edwards says, that at the time when rosewood was first imported, there was on the scale of Custom-house duties, 'Lignum Rhodium, per ton, £40,' referring to the wood from which the oil of Rhodium was extracted, which at that time realized a very high price. The officers claimed the like duty on the furniture rosewood. It was afterwards imported as Jacaranda, Palisander, and Palaxander wood, by which names it is still called on the Continent. The duty was entirely removed, and the consumption has proportionably increased. It is now only known as rosewood, some logs of which have produced as much as £150 when cut into veneers."

Walnut is a handsomely-figured wood, much used for furniture, for which purpose the finest veneers are also employed. Large quantities are still in demand for the manufacture of gunstocks; the prices of which, in the rough, range from a few pence to a couple of guineas each.

Boxwood is an exceedingly hard and useful wood, extensively employed by the turner and the wood-engraver. It is of two kinds, distinguished as Turkey and European boxwood. The former is imported from Constantinople,

Smyrna, and the Black Sea. In size it is very variable, ranging from two and a half to fourteen inches diameter. The colour is generally a deep yellow, sometimes shaded with orange.

Large quantities of boxwood are consumed in the construction of rules, scales, and blocks for engravers, who employ it to the exclusion of all other woods.

The European boxwood does not attain so large a growth, is more curly, softer, and paler than the Turkish. Its usual size is from about one to five inches in diameter. Being stronger than the Turkish box, it is better for lathe-chucks, and will bear more rough usage.

Ebony.—Of this wood there are three varieties, which are usually distinguished by the names of the countries whence they are exported.

The best and most costly of the three is a native of the Mauritius. It is the blackest and hardest, but, unfortunately, the most unsound of the species. The East Indian is the next in order; it is less wasteful, but inferior to the first in grain and colour. The African, which is the last in the list, is the least wasteful, but it is decidedly very poor in colour, and porous in the grain.

Ebony is almost exclusively employed for

turning and ornamental work; flutes, the keys of pianofortes, door-handles, and many similar articles are manufactured from it.

Lime-tree is a clean and light-coloured wood, and quite as easily worked as deal. It requires to be carefully seasoned, otherwise it is very liable to twist and warp, more so than pine. Curriers, shoemakers, &c., use it for their cutting-boards, as it does not influence the course of the knife. It is technically said to be "without grain," as it may be cut with almost equal facility in every direction. Lime-tree is peculiarly free from knots, and, owing to its evenness of texture, is very suitable for carved works. It enters largely into the construction of pianofortes and other musical instruments.

Pear-tree is a brown wood, much used by the Tunbridge turner. In many of its properties it is similar to lime-tree, but harder and tougher. It is largely employed for carved works, and the engraved blocks for calico-printing.

Sycamore is another of the light-coloured woods. When young, it is of a delicate silky white, which changes into a pale brown as the timber becomes old. The wood is strongest when the colour is in the intermediate stage.

Some pieces are beautifully mottled, and are esteemed by the cabinet-maker in the construction of fancy furniture. The plain kinds are made into many articles of domestic utility, such as presses, dairy utensils, &c. It is also a particularly good material of which to make screws.

TABULAR VIEW OF SOME OF THE WOODS IN COMMON USE.

House Carpentry.
Deal.
Oak.
Pine.
Sweet Chestnut.

Strong Framing, &c.
Oak.
Ash.
Beech.
Birch.
Mahogany.

Wet Works, as Piles, Foundations, &c.
Elm.
Oak.
Beech.
Alder.

Joinery and Cabinet Work.
Beech.
Birch.
Cedar.
Pine.

Furniture.
Mahogany.
Rosewood.
Satinwood.
Sandalwood.
Walnut.
Maple.
Black Ebony.
Amboyna.

Foundry Patterns.
Alder.
Deal.
Mahogany.
Pine.

Carpentry and Joinery.

For Turnery (common).	Ornamental Turning.
Alder.	Amboyna.
Aps.	Beefwood.
Beech ⎫ Small.	Black Ebony.
Birch ⎭	Boxwood.
Oak.	Bulletwood.
Elm.	Cocoawood.
Pine.	Coromandel.
Sycamore ⎫ White	Lignum Vitæ.
Holly ⎬ Woods.	Mahogany.
Horse Chestnut ⎭	Maple.
Pear-tree ⎫ Brown	Mustaiba.
Apple-tree ⎬ Woods.	Rosewood.
Plum-tree ⎭	

A comprehensive catalogue of the " Characters and uses of the Woods," will be found in the first volume of Holtzapffel's "Mechanical Manipulation."

CHAPTER IV.

VARIOUS METHODS OF JOINING TIMBER.

THE practical carpenter displays his skill by the judicious choice of that form of connection which will, with the least waste of material, insure the firmest junction of the pieces to be united. He has, moreover, carefully to consider the intensity and direction of the strains tending to rupture the material and separate the joints.

The amateur being principally interested in the construction of light works, it will be unnecessary to investigate very deeply the formation of heavy framing: we shall therefore only notice a few of the most important connections in general use.

When it is necessary permanently to lengthen a beam, another of similar scantling is *pieced* on to it. There are many methods of "piecing" or *scarfing* timber, and every carpenter has his own nostrum, which he considers superior to all others. Considerable ingenuity is often displayed in the various connections required in massive framings, such as roofs, &c., but it is generally found that the simpler forms of attachment are quite as strong as the more elaborate.

The simplest and probably the strongest way of piecing a beam, is to lay the end of one for a certain length over that of the other, and connect them firmly by bolts, which must pass through both timbers. This form of scarfing is certainly clumsy and unartistic, but it is a cheap and serviceable connection, and very good in situations where great neatness is not required.

The next, and probably the most usual kinds of piecing, are shown in fig. 27. In A, the two

Fig. 27.

scantlings to be united are "halved together" by cutting away half the thickness of each of them for the length of the joint, so that when bolted together the beam may appear as one unbroken length. The iron plates are only required at the two extremities of the scarf to keep the ends of the respective timbers from springing under heavy strains. It is necessary to place large iron washers under the nuts, to enable us to screw them up tightly without cutting into the wood.

The form of scarfing represented at B is not so capable of resisting a crushing force as A, which is more suitable for a pillar than B, owing to the support derived from the shoulders, s s. If B were used in a situation where it had to withstand a crushing strain—which tends to force both ends of the beam towards the centre—the wedge-shaped ends would be liable to slide on

Fig. 28.

each other, and the thin tongues, $t\ t$, which confine their extremities, would, owing to the pressure, be apt to split off.

Another method of scarfing is shown in fig. 28. In C the timbers are "halved together" in a somewhat similar manner to A, fig. 27, but the bolts and plates are omitted. The end of each beam has a "rebate," $r\ r$, formed on it, which locks into a corresponding "groove" made in the shoulders. Two keys, $k\ k$, having a slight taper, are driven in to draw the neighbouring parts of the joint closely together. One key in the centre would be equally effective, provided it were made a little wider. This form of connection is capable of resisting either a crushing or a tensile strain, and may be considered the best of the more complicated varieties of piecing. D is not so good, having the same defect as B, fig. 27; and if it were used as a pillar, its strength would be very inferior, owing to the absence of bolts, which are almost necessary in this kind of joint.

If unassisted by iron plates, no form of scarfed tie-beam can possess more than one-third of the

Fig. 29.

strength of the solid beam; and it must be remembered that the strength of any joint or framing can never exceed that of its weakest part.

A very simple kind of scarf much in favour amongst shipwrights is shown in fig. 29, and is termed *fishing* a beam. Two beams of similar scantling are brought end to end, and two pieces of wood, each about half the thickness of the beams, are placed on their opposite sides; the whole is then strongly bolted together. This form of joint is very strong, especially as a post, and it is a ready and effective method of making repairs.

Dovetail connections, as shown in fig. 30, and at E E, fig. 31, are sometimes employed for posts, but they cannot be recommended, and should not be used without plates and bolts, if

Fig. 30.

the weight to be supported is great. Dovetail joints are seldom introduced into heavy carpentry works, even when the grain of both pieces runs in the same direction, as in figs. 30 and 31. When half the thickness of each piece

Fig. 31.

is removed, as at R R, fig. 31 (left-hand figure), and the cut surfaces are brought together, it is called a *lapped* joint. If the timbers be laid so that the grain crosses at a considerable angle the dovetail should not be used, as the shrinkage of the wood will cause the joints to become loose; therefore, D, fig. 32, would be objectionable in a situation where the joint was subjected to even a moderate strain. When the timbers cross at an angle of forty-five degrees they may be united by "halving," as shown at H' H. The method is slightly different

Fig. 32.

in H', where the timbers meet at the ends, and form a corner.

When one timber abuts against another the joint is made as shown at T, in fig. 32. The piece T is called the *tenon*, and the hole, *m*, which is to receive it the *mortise*. The tenon must fit the mortise closely, and its shoulders must rest fairly on the surface of the wood against which it abuts. An oak pin is usually driven in at *p*, to secure the tenon, as it is liable to draw back; the strain should tend to keep the shoulder of the tenon in contact with the wood in which the mortise is made.

The ordinary form of mortise and tenon employed in heavy carpentry is shown to a

Fig. 33.

larger scale in fig. 33. The tenon, T, should seldom exceed one-third of the thickness of the stuff, otherwise the piece containing the mortise, M, will be weaker at that part

Fig. 34.—Tenon-saw.

than the tenon. The endeavour should always be to balance the strength of the two parts, so that, if subjected to a severe strain, they would yield equally. The tenon is formed by cutting away one-third of the thickness of the timber on each side of it, and as the work will receive no further finish than is imparted by the tenon-saw (fig. 34), this tool must be exceedingly well applied to insure a good fit in the mortise. The method of cutting the mortise will be explained hereafter.

After the tenon has been driven home, so that the shoulders, $s\ s'$, bed fairly on the surface of the wood around the mortise—in which they will fail if all the parts be not exactly square—the hole, $p\ p'$, must be bored, but rather smaller than it will ultimately be required. The tenon must then be withdrawn from the mortise, and the hole, p', be enlarged to the proper size for the pin; p must also be increased to the same size, but its centre is removed a trifle towards the shoulders, $s\ s'$, so that when the tenon is re-inserted in the mortise, the holes, $p\ p'$, will not exactly tally. The discrepancy should be very slight, otherwise the tenon may be split when the pin is driven home. By setting the hole in the tenon a little behind that in the mortise, the pin is enabled to draw the tenon forward until both the holes correspond, when the shoulders, $s\ s'$, will bear firmly on the surface, M.

Sometimes the tenon is brought boldly through the mortise, and the pin passed through its extremity. Square pins are used in this situation, being considered less liable to split the end of the tenon. If the end of the tenon be chamfered and the workmanship is good, this form of joint is not unsightly, and is frequently introduced in situations where the joint is exposed to view.

We shall have occasion to speak further of the formation of the tenon and mortise, the dovetail, and some other connections, when explaining the use of the tools employed by the joiner.

CHAPTER V.

SIMPLE WORKS IN WOOD.

WHEN a young fellow enters a carpenter's shop as an apprentice his master will give him plenty of hard initiatory work, which may seem useless and irksome. He will be required to *rip* long pieces of scantling for hours together, and will be kept at this kind of work until he can saw tolerably straight. Perhaps, by way of change, he may be allowed to "rough plane" some boards for coarse works, in which little accuracy is needed.

If the apprentice be careful and work hard, he will soon be relieved of the first drudgery, and be employed on a better class of work. Before he is intrusted with anything important he must assist one of the journeymen, and if he prove intelligent and painstaking, he will soon become a skilled workman.

Thus step by step, beginning at the lowest round of the ladder, must mount all who would achieve real success in any undertaking. One step must be fully mastered before the next is attempted, otherwise much that would have proved of great value remains undiscovered.

Amateurs are rarely good workmen, because they seldom practise sawing and planing sufficiently to become expert.

Many people imagine that complete command of the saw and the plane may be acquired by repairing a piece of furniture, making a box, and similar odd jobs, which, though useful in their way, can afford but little scope for advancement in the joiner's craft.

The amateur joiner has only a narrow field for practice, and unless he make a bold stroke, and combine cabinet-making, his tools will often contract the rust of idleness.

A friend of the author has proved himself a clever amateur cabinet-maker, and can show several pieces of furniture which are exceedingly creditable specimens of art; and one article—a sideboard—deserves special mention, being a handsome and well-finished sample of good workmanship.

We only mention this circumstance to show that amateurs may, if they persevere, become skilled mechanics. That "practice makes perfect" is only true of thoughtful practice. Many men are engaged all their lives at one class of work, and yet never excel. Surely this cannot be for want of practice; no, it is reflection in which they are deficient. The intelligent and thoughtful man feels a pleasure in his work, and is always striving to raise his art to still higher perfection by improving the means at his command, and by endeavouring to devise better and quicker ways of doing the work.

If the plank be required for work in which great accuracy is essential, it will be necessary to be particularly careful when planing the second side to make it exactly parallel to the first; otherwise the plank will not be of uniform thickness throughout. The eye of a skilled workman may be sufficiently "true" or "straight" to enable him to plane up a small piece of stuff without the assistance of a line or other artificial guide. A beginner, however, must not attempt to work in this way, or he will invariably spoil whatever he undertakes. Next to the square, the marking-gauge is the workman's best safeguard; the straight-edge should also be at hand, its aid being indispensable for testing the truth of extensive flat surfaces, as well as long narrow ones.

After the rough outside of the plank has been removed, the surface should be "tried up," or generally planed over with the trying-plane, to make it tolerably flat. If the longitudinal edges of the plank be very uneven, they must also be "roughly shot." The marking-gauge must be adjusted to the thickness to which the work is to be planed. If the wood will "hold up," say to one inch thick, the head of the gauge must be set back one inch from the scoring point. The plank must be raised and supported on one edge, the head of the gauge being forcibly applied to, and moved along, the true surface, while the scoring point leaves a clear line on the uppermost edge, and as much below the rough untouched surface as the substance of the work now exceeds the finished thickness to which the gauge is set. Both the longitudinal edges must be gauged, and the ends also, if they be tolerably straight and smooth. If the second side be now carefully planed down to the lines, we shall have a plank of uniform thickness. While planing the last side, the straight-edge must be frequently applied across the work to give us timely notice, if we be removing too much in the centre. It is a safe plan to plane down the surface near the edges to within a little of the gauge-lines, and then to remove the stuff towards the centre, remembering to use the straight edge frequently in the cross direction, and also occasionally lengthwise. When the second side has been made as true as the first, and the thickness is found to be uniform, the edges and the ends must be completed as before explained.

The process is somewhat different for thick

works. After the first side has been "tried up," one of the edges is planed at right angles to it, the truth being tested by the square, the stock of which is applied to the first side, and the blade to the edge. Great care must be taken to make the edge or right-angled side—as it may be considered in thick work—exactly square to the first, as these two surfaces are required to serve as the foundations from which the remaining sides are to be wrought. The gauge must now be set to the finished thickness or the distance which is to exist between the first side and the one opposite or parallel to it.

The first side, which we will call A, and the adjacent edge or right-angled side, B, should be marked by a pencil line extending from one to the other, that we may distinguish them from the two remaining surfaces, C and D, which are to be wrought from them. The second side, C, when planed to within a little of the gauge-lines, may be tested by the square, the stock resting on the edge, B, and the blade on C. The square must be applied at short intervals as the work approaches towards completion, and should be moved over the entire surface, as some parts may be out of square, though closely bordering on others which are true.

The sides, A, B, and C, are now supposed to be finished; it therefore only remains to operate on

D to complete the work. The edge or fourth side, D, might be planed at right angles to the first side, A, by the assistance of the square, if it were not required to be also parallel to the second side, B.

We made A and C parallel to each other; the same relation must therefore exist between B and D, to render the work correct. The marking-gauge must be set to the new measure, the width or distance required between the edges—the head being rubbed against B, while the point marks out the new surface, D. Two lines must be scored—one on A, the other on C—to guide us in planing the edge square to them.

If the work has been properly executed, the sides will prove equally true when tried by the square in any direction. Sometimes the several surfaces will appear true in the order of their formation, but on reversing the test they will no longer agree. This want of accuracy can occasionally be traced to the square, which may not be in good order, but more frequently the fault rests with the workman.

Squaring and planing-up works are not easy of accomplishment, and even the simplest works require considerable skill to achieve satisfactorily, and constant practice is necessary to insure success.

We must suppose our pupils to have only

commenced their apprenticeship, and shall therefore begin with the mere rudiments of the joiner's art.

The construction of a plain deal box is probably the simplest work our pupils could select for their first attempt. The wood for the "carcase" of the box having been cut out and planed in accordance with the directions already given, the sides may now be glued or nailed together. Before detailing the method of "glueing up" works, however, a few words respecting the choice of the glue may be useful to our readers.

The best glue is prepared from parings of the hides of animals, previously to the process of tanning. The quality of the glue may be tested in several ways. The superior kinds are of a pale brown colour, and devoid of taste or smell. When held between the eye and the light the cake of glue should appear semi-transparent, and entirely free from cloudy or black spots, which indicate the presence of foreign matter. If a large quantity of glue is to be purchased, it will be advisable to take a sample, and subject it to a severe trial. The glue must be broken into small pieces, and placed in a vessel with sufficient cold water to cover it. If, after the lapse of three or four days, the glue swell powerfully without melting, it may be considered the best quality.

In dry weather a cake of glue is generally crisp and hard, but it is liable to become soft in a moist atmosphere. If the glue be soft in dry weather it should be rejected, being probably of inferior quality.

The kettle in which the glue is melted for use consists of two vessels, one within the other, a certain space existing between them for a water-bath to determine the temperature, which can never exceed that of boiling water. This provision is absolutely necessary to save the glue from being unduly heated or burnt, whereby its adhesive properties would be destroyed.

It is a good plan to allow the glue to soak in cold water for several hours before placing the kettle on the fire. The kettle must not be put on a fierce fire, but should be suffered to simmer gently on the hob, until the glue is thoroughly melted. A cover should be provided to exclude the dust, a notch being made in the edge for a stick or brush, with which the glue may be occasionally stirred. If too thick, a little of the hot water contained in the larger vessel may be added to the glue, which should be sufficiently thin to run in a fine stream from the brush. Shortly before removing the kettle the water may be allowed to boil gently, to ensure the glue being of sufficiently high temperature to remain fluid until the neighbouring portions of the work to be united are properly adjusted. The strength of common glue may be somewhat increased by adding a small portion of finely-powdered chalk, which must be thoroughly incorporated with it. Another preparation which will resist moisture is made by melting one pound of the best glue in two quarts of skimmed milk.

A very strong glue of great service for uniting small mouldings and other separate portions of work which are liable, owing to their small surface, to become detached from the main body, may be made thus:—Dissolve one ounce of the best isinglass, by gentle heat, in a pint of water, and strain it through a piece of cloth. The isinglass must now be placed in a glue-kettle with the best cake glue, which has been soaking for twenty-four hours in cold water. A gill of the strongest vinegar must be added, and the whole allowed to melt slowly near the fire. The mixture must be stirred occasionally to ensure the complete incorporation of the ingredients. The glue may be suffered to boil up once, after which the impurities must be strained off, and the cement left to cool. If the kettle be wanted for ordinary glue, the "strong glue" may be poured on a slab of stone to cool, after which the cake so formed can be broken into pieces of a convenient size for use.

Having ascertained that the four pieces of which the "carcase" of the box is to be constructed are quite square, and fit truly to each other, they must be marked, so that their proper relationship may be known when "glueing up" is commenced.

To ensure a good and firm joint it is necessary to have the glue very fluid, and as hot as the water-bath of the kettle can make it. It is also of equal importance to bring the pieces which are to be united as nearly in contact as possible, thereby excluding the superabundant cement which would otherwise prevent the close union of the parts.

If the top of the bench be uneven a flat board should be placed on it, otherwise some difficulty may be experienced in glueing the box together truly square. One of the sides of the "carcase" must be laid on the board with the inner side upwards, and the end pieces, which have respectively been glued on one extremity, are rubbed firmly down on it, in order to exclude the surplus glue and bring the wood into close contact. The opposite extremities of the ends are next glued, and the second side is pressed forcibly upon them.

It will be found that the cross-grain of the end pieces quickly absorbs the glue, therefore its application must be repeated several times before the usual quantity will remain on the surface. Glue will never hold so strongly in the cross as in the length-way of the grain, consequently little reliance can be placed on the strength of a box in which the cross-grain of the end pieces is merely glued to the sides.

The four sides of the box or "carcase" being "glued up," it must be turned over to ascertain if the edges of the side and end pieces rest fairly on the board; and if at all distorted the "carcase" must be corrected as quickly as possible, while the glue is soft, as any disturbance after the glue begins to set will be fatal to the soundness of the joint. The work may be bound together more closely by screw-clamps, which will also tend to preserve its shape while drying. After the clamps have been adjusted the truth of the work must be again tested, not only on the edges, but also by a square applied from the sides, to discover if the ends be at right angles to them. Before leaving the work to dry, the waste glue which has oozed out at the joints should be removed by a bit of sponge slightly moistened with the hot water in the kettle. If the waste glue were allowed to harden, it would not only be difficult to remove, but would stain the work and give it an unworkmanlike appearance.

The work must not be disturbed for at least

four-and-twenty hours, and if the weather be damp, a longer period should be allowed.

When the glue is thoroughly hard the clamps may be removed and the bottom of the box attached. If, on examination, the edges of the "carcase" prove not exactly "fair," they must be dressed carefully by the smoothing-plane, until the bottom fits them closely all round.

Glueing on the bottom of the box is merely a repetition of the process we have just described. It may be found more convenient to keep the bottom closely in contact with the "carcase" while the glue is drying, by a couple of weights instead of the screw-clamps which were used for the sides. After the carcase has been rubbed down firmly on the bottom and the waste glue removed, the box may either be turned upside down, so that the weights may be placed on the bottom, or, being undisturbed, the weights may be supported by a piece of wood placed on the box as a temporary cover.

As the box, however carefully glued together, will require to be finally "finished off" by the smoothing-plane, it will somewhat facilitate the process to allow the extremities of the side pieces to project a very small amount beyond the ends. The bottom may also with advantage be a trifle larger than the exterior dimensions of the carcase. If the work be quite true, and the glueing is well performed, no perceptible provision for the final finish will be required.

Great care must be taken in the finishing to avoid "spalling off" the wood when planing the cross-grain ends of the side pieces. The plane must be used obliquely, and not for the entire length or depth of the ends, the endeavour being to work alternately from the upper and lower edges towards the middle, where the opposite cuts will meet and balance each other.

If we require a board of considerable width, it will be necessary to glue two or more narrow planks edge to edge. To do this successfully the edges of the respective planks which are to be united must be exactly straight and square across. When one of the edges has been carefully shot according to the indications of the "straight-edge," it may in its turn be used as a straight-edge in working the edge of the plank with which it is to be united. If a little chalk be rubbed evenly all over the true edge, a small portion of the white powder will be deposited on the prominent points of the work, if the former be slightly moved backwards and forwards over the latter in the direction of its length. By removing the material where the chalk has adhered we shall soon bring the edge of the second plank into close contact with that of the first.

When about to glue the boards together one of

the pieces must be fixed vertically in the chops of the bench, the lower end being raised a few inches from the floor. The second plank must also be placed in an upright position, and supported by a block of wood at the same height as the first, against which it is allowed to rest obliquely, so that the edges to be glued may form a slight angle with each other. The glue-brush is now run up and down the angle formed by the edges of the boards, and when the cement has been thoroughly worked into the grain of the wood, the edge of the second plank must be brought in contact with that of the first, which is firmly secured in chops of the bench. The second board, which is held by the joiner, must be pressed and rubbed forcibly against the first until the joint begins to feel stiff under the hand, when the plank must be brought into its proper position. A straight-edge should be applied across the face of the board to test its accuracy before removing it from the bench. If the edges which we have just glued together be not exactly square across, the board will prove rounding on one side and hollow on the other. A similar discrepancy may be occasioned by the respective edges of the planks not "bedding" fairly on each other. A critical examination of each side of the board will enable us to discover any such fault, which may be rectified by pressing the plank so as to close the open joint. If the joint appear quite sound, or if the closing of a gap fail to make the work flat, the joint must be separated and rectified by the plane. As such a proceeding would be very unsatisfactory, and waste much time, the greatest care must be taken when shooting the edges to ensure their accuracy. If the work be accurate, the joint must be sponged over to remove the waste glue, and after allowing a few minutes for the glue to set, the board may be carefully removed from the bench by two people, and rested in an inclined position against the wall of the workshop.

When a truly flat board of considerable width is required it would be unwise to employ one plank, even supposing we could find a piece of sufficiently large growth suitable for our purpose. We have already stated that the woods are very liable to warp and become otherwise distorted in the cross-way of the grain, consequently little dependence can be placed on the material in this direction. It should not, therefore, if unassisted, be employed of great width in works where permanence of form is important. It will frequently be found that the plank becomes convex on the side which was towards the centre of the tree, provided both sides are subjected to similar conditions.

If the wide plank be cut into several narrow

ones and the alternate pieces be reversed, and then glued up edge to edge, the wide plank thus formed will retain its shape much better than it could have done in its natural state. A wide plank not artificially formed would become curved, like a large bow, one side being convex and the other concave. But in a " made-up plank," the component parts being comparatively narrow, the curvature is shorter, and changing the sides of the alternate pieces has the effect of imparting a slightly serpentine outline instead of a large curve to the surface of the work, if it become warped.

Since the direction in which the wood is employed is of so much importance, it may be observed that those parts upon which the most reliance is placed to retain the work in shape should always be constructed in the length-way of the grain. For instance, the length and width of a box are usually much greater than its depth, and as the true figure of the work depends on the permanence of the side and end pieces, their longest directions must be made *with* the grain. If all the dimensions of the box be equal, the length-way of the grain must still be at right angles to the depth of the box. The grain of the end pieces must always be in the same direction, or plain, as that of the sides; the combination of the four pieces will then mutually support and retain each other in shape.

The liability to warp is not removed by changing the alternate sides of the narrow pieces or strips into which the wide plank was divided,

Fig. 35.

and although the evil may be mitigated to some extent by this treatment, yet we must resort to the more powerful restraints of *clamps* to retain the work in shape. The simplest forms of clamp are shown in fig. 35, which may be supposed to represent the ordinary drawing-board used by mechanical draughtsmen. The board is constructed of two pine planks, A B, free from knots, and thoroughly seasoned. The edges which are to be united must be very truly planed, and a shallow groove formed in each for the reception of a thin strip of wood, t, called a *slip-feather*, which materially strengthens the joint. The groove cannot be satisfactorily made without a *grooving-plane*, of which we shall speak presently. In the absence of this tool the joint may be sufficiently well made for ordinary purposes, by simply glueing the edges together.

When the glue is thoroughly hard, the board must be planed upon the sides and edges. The clamp, C C, which is made of a well-seasoned straight-grained piece of " stuff " is fastened by screws across the grain of the board a short distance from the end. It is always necessary to have two clamps—one near each extremity of the board,—and if the length of the latter be considerable, a third clamp may be required in the centre. As the board is liable to shrink or become narrower, it is subjected to a considerable strain by being rigidly fixed to the clamp, C C, which is incapable of shrinking in the direction of its length. The clamp being unable to yield in the length-way of the grain, it can afford no liberty to the cross-grained wood of the board, which is apt to split and tear away from the fastenings by which it is confined.

A better kind of clamp which effectually preserves the truth of the board, and at the same time allows it to contract without restraint, is seen at D D. Instead of securing the clamps by screws or other rigid connections, a dovetail, d, is formed on the side next the board, in which latter is made a corresponding dovetail groove. The dovetail on the clamp and the groove in the board are made with a slight taper in the length-way to enable the clamp to draw itself tight when driven forward. The board is quite free to shrink throughout the entire length of the dovetail, and the truth of the surface is also strictly maintained. If the shrinking of the board be so considerable as to loosen the clamp, it may be immediately tightened by a few light blows of a hammer on the wide end of the dovetail. This form of clamp is very superior to the one first named, but it is much more difficult to make; for if the dovetail be badly fitted, it will fail to afford the requisite support to the board. The clamp, C C, is a very ready and convenient device for strengthening the covers, and also the bottoms and sides of rough boxes or packing-cases.

Fig. 36 represents a wide board formed by narrow strips glued edge to edge. This board is strengthened by a clamp, E E, which is secured to the end instead of the side. The ends of the board (only one is shown) are *rebated* on each side to form the tongue, T, which should be one-third of the thickness of the material.

Fig. 36.

A groove is planed in the edge of the clamp, E E, to receive the tongue, which should fit it moderately tight. If there be any doubt respecting the complete seasoning of the wood of which the board is constructed, it would be imprudent to glue the clamp to the board, except in the middle of its length. The shrinking of the pieces on either side of the middle strip would occasion sufficient contraction in the width of the board to cause it to separate from the glue which bound it to the clamp. This description of clamp is much used in cabinet-work, and as the seasoning is then tolerably complete, the work may be glued throughout with little fear of subsequent failure.

This clamp is frequently employed for strengthening and retaining in shape the light covers of boxes, office writing-desks, &c. The board, W, will not be required of large dimensions for the purposes named; and if mahogany be used, it will be unnecessary to "make up" by glueing strips together. If a surface of several feet in extent be required, a frame consisting of four or more parts is constructed, and small thin boards, called *panels*, are introduced to fill the vacancies between the several members of the frame. The doors and shutters of a house are examples of this description of framing, which is in very general use. All the vertical or longest pieces of the frame are called the *styles*, and the cross bars which connect them the *rails*.

The extremities of the rails are usually formed into tenons, which lodge in mortises made in the styles. A groove for the reception of the panel is worked in the styles and rails. The panel should not fit the groove too closely, or it will not have sufficient liberty for expansion and contraction, which, if resisted, will cause the wood to split. The mouldings, when not worked out of the solid, are secured to the styles and rails, and the panels are still unrestrained.

The formation of framed and panelled works can scarcely be considered as easy examples of joinery; we must therefore reserve this subject for future investigation.

It is often necessary to glue a narrow strip on the edge of a board to receive a moulding, &c., in which case it is better to make the addition wider than it will ultimately be required, and when the glue is hard, to cut off the excess of material. By this means we are enabled to make a sounder joint, as the strip is less liable to spring up at the ends, if its width be equal to about three or four times its thickness.

It is sometimes necessary to form a large curve or sweep either by bending the wood, or by cutting it to the required shape. If the sweep be large, bending the material is the most economical process. The simplest but certainly not the strongest method of bending is performed by making several kerfs with the tenon-saw along the edge which is required to yield or stretch. The kerfs must be equi-distant and of uniform depth, and care must be taken when bending not to cripple the work by applying too much force.

When the desired curve is obtained, the ends of the sweep should be confined by securing them to the board on which the work must be laid for glueing. The edge in which the saw kerfs were made being now convex, the kerfs will be found much wider than they were previously to bending the wood. The strength of the work may be considerably increased by filling the cuts with glue and inserting thin wedges, which will also tend to preserve the curvature of the sweep. Sometimes a strip of canvass is glued upon the edge in which the cuts have been made. A nice curve cannot be formed when the outer edge is nicked, as the wood will yield unequally.

If the wood of which the sweep is to be made be not too thick and rigid, it may sometimes be bent by soaking the side which is to be convex with hot water, at the same time exposing the opposite side to the fire. If the work be fixed while hot, it will retain when cold the form thus impressed upon it.

When curved work is required of considerable substance it is usual to build it up by glueing several thicknesses, one upon another, in a *caul*, or mould, formed of two pieces of hard wood, which have been cut to the proper sweep for our work. The wood of which the curve is to be formed must be even in grain, free from knots, and of uniform thickness.

For some purposes, especially in pattern-making, it is convenient to cut several pieces of the required curve out of comparatively thin "stuff," and to glue them together till the proper thickness is obtained. If the sweep be formed by joining several short pieces end to end, the second layer must be arranged so that the joints shall occur midway between those of the lower course or in the centre of the short pieces. It is easy to perceive that if the joints in the several layers were placed directly in a line, the work could have very little strength; it is therefore necessary to "break joints," as in building a brick wall.

We shall have occasion to speak further respecting the process of "glueing up" works, when considering the construction, various framings, veneering, &c.

Although glue is very largely employed as a means of uniting many portions of the work, yet the carpenter, joiner, and even the cabinet-maker, would be unable, without the assistance of nails and screws, to ensure the requisite strength of those parts which are subjected to severe strains.

In fig. 37 several varieties of nails in general use are shown, but without reference to their size.

1. A form called *rose-sharp*, largely employed

for rough purposes, such as coopering, fencing, and general out-door works, is very suitable for driving into hard wood. Another kind termed *fine-rose* are used for pine and similar soft woods, and being thinner than the former sort is less liable to split the material. The head of each variety is large and spreading, and very good for holding the work down.

2. This nail, also distinguished as *rose*, has a *flat* or *chisel* point, which is less likely to split

Fig. 37.

the wood than one with a sharp extremity. The chisel edge is placed across the grain, and the danger of spoiling the work by even a slight tendency to split, is avoided, and a nail of this description generally holds more firmly than those with sharp points.

3. The *clasp* nail is largely used by house carpenters in deal and other soft woods. The name is derived from the peculiar formation of the

head, which slopes abruptly on opposite sides, clasps the wood when driven into it, and when punched below the surface, the plane can be used over it without being injured.

4. The *clout* is used for nailing iron and other metal work to wood. The head is flat and circular, and the shank round, terminating in a sharp point.

5. *Counterclout* nails have "countersinks," or conical necks, under their heads, which are required to lie level or flush with the surface of the work; the shanks are round with chisel points. These nails are principally used by smiths and wheelwrights.

6. *Fine dog* is distinguished from a stouter nail of a similar kind, called *strong* or *weighty dog*. Both sorts are used for fastening down strong iron-work, and for many other purposes in which the heads, which are very solid and slightly countersunk, are not required to lie level with the surface of the work. The shanks are round, and terminate in spear points, which are well adapted for piercing and clenching.

7. *Kent-hurdle* nails have broad and rather thin-rose heads, clean drawn shanks with good spear points, which are very favourable for nailing and clenching the oaken bars of hurdles together. A description called *gate nails* is somewhat similar.

8. *Rose-clench* are nails much employed by ship and boat-builders. They are termed clench, because, after being driven through the plank, their ends are bent over by the hammer or clenched. If additional security and neatness be required, a small diamond-shape plate, *r*, called a *rove*, is slipped over the point, which is then rivetted down upon it, thereby drawing the planks very closely together. The nail is used extensively for securing the wood-sheathing to ships' sides, for which purpose it is unsurpassed, as the square blunt end punches the hole, which would require to be bored, if a pointed nail were used, owing to the fragile nature of the wood, which is very liable to split. Large quantities of these nails are consumed in the construction of rough boxes, packing-cases, and other coarse works, for which time cannot be spared to bore holes for the nails.

9. *Horse nails*, employed for attaching the shoe to the hoof. Formerly the nails were made with square heads, but the preference was given to the shape represented, which is also slightly countersunk, to allow the heads to lie in the groove made for them in the shoe.

10. *Brads* are very useful nails, great in demand for all varieties of light joinery work. The amateur will probably use this class of nails

almost to the exclusion of any other; they are little liable to split the wood and hold well.

The best nails are made of wrought iron, of which the toughest description is selected, especially for *clench* nails. Large quantities of cheap nails are manufactured from cast iron, which is annealed to lessen its brittleness. Malleable cast-iron nails answer very well for numerous coarse purposes, such as nailing up laths for partitions, for securing fruit trees to garden walls, and many similar works in which much strength is not required.

It is not so easy to drive a nail properly as many people imagine. If the head of the nail be not struck fairly in the centre, but obliquely, the shank will either be bent or knocked out of the true position, to which it cannot without some difficulty be again restored. If the wood be hard and the nail long and slender, the liability to bend or cripple the shank is considerable. The best way to avoid this is to bore a hole slightly smaller than the shank is in the middle of its length, if it be taper, and if parallel, a little less than the part immediately above the point. It is evident that if the hole be made as large as the nail, the latter can have little or no hold, and if too small, the relief which it affords is insufficient to avert the danger of either splitting the wood or crippling the nail.

When nailing two pieces of hard wood together, it is only necessary for the nail to fit tightly, or hold in the piece which receives the point, the hole in the wood which is to be secured being sufficiently large to allow the nail to pass through easily. By this means the labour of driving a large nail is much relieved, and the shank is well supported if the wood be moderately thick. It is unnecessary to bore a hole for the nail in deal and other soft woods, except as a precautionary measure, when there is danger of splitting the material. If several nails are to be driven in a row near the edge or end of a board, as in nailing the sides to the ends of a box, it would be prudent to make small holes, which would probably not only save the wood from splitting, but also direct the nails which might otherwise go astray. Nothing looks worse, or less artistic, than the protruding points of several nails which have broken through the side of the work owing to crooked driving. The thinner the wood of which the box is constructed, the greater is the difficulty of avoiding the disfigurement of projecting points, and increased care must be bestowed in driving the nails straight.

To use the hammer properly, the shaft or handle must be firmly grasped in the right hand, and so near the extremity that only about an inch of the shaft projects below the little finger. If a few very light blows or taps be required, the shaft may be held shorter or nearer the head; but this is not the legitimate way of handling the tool. Before striking a blow the face of the hammer should be rubbed on the floor, or on a board sprinkled with a little powdered chalk, to remove any grease that may adhere to it, which would cause the hammer to glance off the head of the nail. Though the shaft be held near the extremity, the hammer is perfectly under control, and it should be used lightly at first, gradually increasing the force of the blows as the nail sinks into the wood.

If the blows be violent at first, the nail will be bent or sent astray, as at this time it derives very little support from the wood into which it is being driven. The endeavour should be to increase the force of the blows at intervals, as the nail seems able to bear it, as a too sudden change from light and rapid blows to heavy strokes is almost sure to send the nail astray. The *aim* should be accurate, and the head of the nail must be struck by the centre of the hammer-face, otherwise it may be spoilt by a blow from the edge, which would also very probably bend the shank. Sometimes the greatest care will fail to ensure the straight driving of the nail. If the nail appear disposed to bend or go astray, it may frequently be restored to its proper position by a few well-directed and slightly oblique blows, which must be applied on the side of the head furthest from the place which the nail should occupy.

Occasionally the pincers (fig. 38) must be used to extract a nail which has become hopelessly crippled. If the nail be very fast, as it often is in hard wood, one of the bows of the pincers

Fig. 38.

must be allowed to rest on the surface of the work, in order that it may act as the fulcrum of a lever when the handles, which must be grasped in the right hand, are powerfully depressed. A double claw is provided at the end of one of the handles for " prizing up " nails which have been home. The claws are sharp enough to penetrate the wood around and under the head of the nail, the neck of which can then pass between them. By depressing the opposite end of the pincers the nail will be raised sufficiently to enable us to draw it out.

If the work require a finishing touch from the plane, the heads of the nails must be punched below the surface. This is almost equally necessary if the wood is to be painted, and the cavities left by the displaced heads must be filled with putty to hide them. The punch consists of a cylindrical piece of steel about three inches long, tapering from the middle of its length to one extremity. The point must be quite blunt, otherwise it will not drive the nail down satisfactorily. Two opposite sides of the taper end of the punch must be flat for *brads*, and somewhat similar in shape to the nail itself. The point of the punch must be hardened to enable it to retain its shape. If the end be heated to a dull red, and then be thrust into a lump of tallow or candle-grease, it will become sufficiently hard.

The *wood screw*, also sometimes called the *screwnail*, is a strong and ready means of uniting numerous works in wood. The screw possesses a great advantage over the nail in situations where considerable strength is required, as it powerfully resists any tendency to draw it out of the wood like a common nail. There are many instances in joinery and cabinet making, in which a nail would be useless, owing to the fragile character of the work and the trifling thickness of the material, which could not afford sufficient hold for a nail. It is in these delicate articles that the screw proves of so much value. The screw, unlike the nail, needs no application

Carpentry and Joinery. 107

of the hammer, which is another advantage peculiar to the former. The jar occasioned by driving a nail would be fatal to some of the lighter classes of works, supposing nail-hold could be found in them.

Probably Mr. Nettleford's patent screw represented at A, fig. 39, is the best at present manufactured. The upper side of the "thread," which is flat and considerably inclined, offers great re-

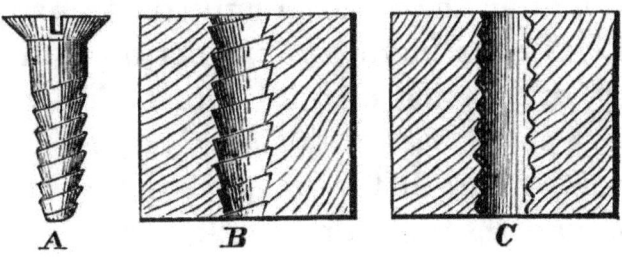

Fig. 39.

sistance to the screw being drawn out of the wood like a common nail. The thread may be compared to a cone, the base of which stands upwards. The conical or sloping sides of the thread enable the screw to penetrate the wood with great facility. The stem or shank of the screw is also made taper, being smaller at the extremity than at the commencement of the thread. At B is shown the mould or impression made by the screw in wood; and at C is seen the irregular and imperfect counterpart of the thread of a common wood-screw. Nettleford's patent screw may not be sold by the tradesman with whom some of our readers may be obliged to deal; however, the best specimens of the ordinary screws will answer sufficiently well for many purposes.

When choosing either iron or brass wood-screws select those with moderately deep threads, approaching as nearly as possible the shape of A, fig. 39. The end or point of the screw must also be smaller than the blank part just below the head. Those having a projecting bur at the extremity of the thread should be rejected, as the bur is apt to tear away the wood as the screw advances, leaving little or perhaps nothing by which it can hold. The nick, or diametrical saw-cut made in the head for the screw-driver, must be of uniform depth, and not, as it frequently happens, highest at the centre. The depth of the nick is also of some importance, for if too deep the head is liable to be broken by the screw-driver, which latter, however, will have insufficient hold if the nick be too shallow. The depth of the nick may with advantage be about half the thickness of the head, and it should be of the same width throughout.

The end of the screw-driver should be formed as shown in the two views, fig. 40. The sloping sides, or chamfers, must not meet at the extremity, or a sharp edge will result, which would injure the sides of the nick if the screw-driver slipped out. The chamfers must be ground to an angle of about ten or fifteen degrees, or the tool will be unable to retain its hold in the nick, and by frequently slipping out it will not only disfigure the head of the screw, but also lessen

Fig. 40.

our power to move it. For very large wood-screws, and for screws for metal work, the extremity of the driver should be somewhat differently formed, as seen in fig. 41. The sloping sides, or chamfers, are unfavourable in their action when much resistance has to be overcome,

Fig. 41.

as the pressure on the inclined surface is apt to force the tool out of the nick. In fig. 41 the sides of the driver are filled parallel for a short distance, to enable it to fit the nick for its entire depth. The parallel part must not be deeper than necessary, or it will be liable to break; and for the same reason a sharp angle or corner should be avoided where the straight part meets the chamfer. The end must be made of steel, and hardened, so that a smooth file will just scratch it. There is less difficulty in driving a screw straight than a nail, as the former will generally follow the direction of the hole made to receive it, while the latter is influenced in a great measure by the blows of the hammer.

A hole must be made for the screw, but not larger than is absolutely necessary, as any excess of size will rob the screw of a part of its hold. There is, however, danger of splitting the wood if the hole be too small; and sometimes the screw, after entering a short distance, "strips" the thread or hold it had obtained, and requires to be replaced by one of larger size. This is very likely to occur if the wood be hard and brittle, as the point of the screw drives the fibre of the wood before it, and contracts the hole so much that the slight hold the screw has obtained is insufficient to enable it to overcome the resistance. The hole should be as nearly as possible the size of the screw at the *bottom* of the thread, and if made in hard wood the material must be removed by a gimlet like fig. 42, if the hole be small, and if large, by a *twisted gimlet*, fig. 44. Very small screws require so little room that, generally speaking, the hole for them may be made by a brad-awl, which is also used for making holes in soft wood like deal, &c., the fibre being so yielding that it is unnecessary to remove it, as it may be so easily displaced.

Fig. 42.   Fig. 43.   Fig. 44.

It is necessary when screwing two pieces of wood together to make the hole in the piece which receives the head sufficiently large to allow the screw to slip through easily. The head of the screw must be let into the wood by removing the "stuff" round the edge of the hole by a *counter-sink bit*, fig. 43. The counter-sink should only be deep enough to suffer the head to lie fairly on a level with the surface of the work. In the absence of a counter-sink bit the edge of the hole must be pared away by a chisel.

A little tallow rubbed over the threads of the screw will greatly facilitate its progress, and also preserve it from rust, which powerfully opposes any future attempt to remove the screw. In the act of unscrewing, the downward pressure on the screw-driver should be only sufficient to keep the tool in the nick, otherwise the thread in the wood will be strained, and perhaps stripped, by the needless resistance it has to overcome. Considerable pressure may be required to keep the screw-driver in the nick when endeavouring to start a screw which is very firmly fixed; but no injury is occasioned at this time, as the entire length of the thread in the wood is sustaining the resistance.

We have endeavoured to point out the difficulties which are likely to arise where nails and

Fig. 45.

screws are employed, and to suggest the best remedies in each case; but as practice alone can enable our readers to avoid casualties incidental to amateur workmanship, we will leave this subject and consider some of the tools of which we have not yet spoken.

The *table, compass,* or *lock-saw* (fig. 45), is used for cutting out curved or sweep work. In general formation it is similar to the hand-saw (fig. 2), of which it may be considered a diminutive copy. The blade is sufficiently narrow near the extremity to enable it to follow a curve of two or three inches radius.

A somewhat similar but more delicate instrument is met with in the *key-hole* or *fret-saw* (fig. 46). The blade of this saw is thinner and

Fig. 46.

more flexible than that of the table-saw, and is fixed in the handle by two set screws which can be slackened by an ordinary screw-driver. A narrow slot penetrates the handle in the direction of its length, through which the blade can pass, so that it may be shortened or lengthened at pleasure, to suit the character of the work in hand. This provision is necessary to save the blade from being bent or broken when the point is used.

Neither of these saws is capable of withstanding rough usage, and if they stick fast in the work must be carefully extricated. These saws do not always make their first incision at the edge of the wood, but sometimes in the middle of a board; consequently, a hole must be bored at one, and occasionally at both ends of the intended skerf, for the introduction and removal of the saw. Most of the curved works that amateurs are likely to attempt may be executed by these tools.

For some purposes, however, a very fine saw-kerf may be necessary, and the curve is perhaps too small for either the table or the key-hole saw.

In this case the *turning saw* (fig. 47) would be wanted. The blade is so slight and flexible that it cannot be driven forward by one end in the

Fig. 47.

usual manner, and must necessarily be stretched in a wooden frame, to impart sufficient rigidity to enable it to act satisfactorily. The extremities of the blade are secured by pins to round handles which are formed with circular necks fitting stiffly into the lower ends of the frame.

The two end-pieces or *side-rails, a, b, c, d,* which form the principal members of the frame, are kept apart by the cross-bar or *stretcher, e f,* the ends of which penetrate a short distance into them, but are not secured, as the side rails are required to rotate slightly on their extremities. To the top of the frame, at *a c*, is secured a coil of cord which is twisted by a lever (*g*) until, by shortening, it contracts the top of the frame and expands the lower extremity, thus imparting the requisite degree of tension to the saw. The circular necks of the handles are longer than the thickness of the frame, and diametrical slots or kerfs are made in the projecting portions (*n n*) for the reception of the ends of the blade, which are secured by small pins, one in each neck. One extremity of the blade must be disconnected from its handle if the saw cannot be introduced or withdrawn at the margin of the work. The frame, by slightly rotating on the circular necks, can assume any angle which convenience of handling or the outline of the work may require, and without affecting the course of the saw.

Fig. 34 represents the *tenon, sash, carcase,* and *dove-tail* saws, which may be spoken of collectively as *back-saws*. The tenon saw is the largest, and the dove-tail the smallest of the group. These saws derive their distinctive titles from the description of the work for which they are employed.

The *sawing-block* is much used for guiding the back-saws when cutting the extremities of mouldings, or the separate parts of light frames to a mitre joint. The block is formed like a trough with open ends. The sides must be quite parallel, both inside and out, and three saw-kerfs are very carefully cut in them with the back-saw. The kerfs near the right-hand extremity of the block are exactly opposite each other, consequently the saw will move in them at right angles to the sides, and cut the ends of the work square. The other kerfs are made at angles of 45 degrees, and slope in opposite directions for cutting mitres at the ends of pieces which are to be united at right angles. If the kerfs be not exactly vertical, they are worse than useless, as the saw is constrained to follow their inaccuracies, which are imparted to the work.

To use the sawing-block, it is only necessary to place the work inside, holding it firmly against the further side, with the pencil-mark indicating the line of division exactly opposite the kerf. The saw must be used with care, to avoid widening the kerfs in the block.

When several pieces of equal length are to be cut off, a small block of wood, called a stop, is temporarily attached to the sawing-block, which thus saves the labour of measuring and marking out, at the same time ensuring greater accuracy. The "shooting-boards," represented on pages 48 and 49, are sometimes used in lieu of the sawing-block.

Carpentry and Joinery. 117

The kerfs for the guidance of the saw are made in the "strip," and the work is supported on the "bed." This arrangement is very convenient when it is necessary to saw the ends of the work immediately after "shooting its edges."

The spokeshave (fig. 48) is somewhat similar in its action to the plane; but owing to the absence of the guide principle which exists in the "sole" of a plane, it cannot be employed

Fig. 48.

for working flat surfaces, as it descends into all the inequalities, instead of removing them. This tool may be compared to a knife held at a very low inclination, and indeed the pitch is lower than that of any of the surfacing planes, being only about 25 or 30 degrees. The spokeshave works well in the direction of the grain, but it is only applicable to small rounded or curved works which cannot be wrought by the plane. The blade is usually secured to the stock or handle by two spikes or tangs which fit tightly into the wood. Set screws, s, s (fig. 48) are sometimes employed to facilitate the adjustment of the blade, which must be regulated as carefully as an ordinary plane-iron. The extremities of the stock are rounded into convenient handles, which are grasped in right and left hands respectively. The operator applies the tool to the work with the edge of the cutter towards him, and removes shavings by drawing the instrument forward.

While speaking of the various tools used in carpentry and joinery, we may observe that the

Fig. 49.

firmer chisel (fig. 4) varies in width from about $\frac{1}{16}$ inch to $2\frac{1}{2}$ inches, and is generally used for finishing portions of the work which may have been left rough or ill-defined from the saw, &c.

If the work be light, it is held down on the bench by the left hand, and the chisel is applied by the right. The flat side of the chisel is placed next the work, with which it must form a slight angle, to enable the edge to penetrate the wood. When the work is large or heavy, it must be fixed either by the " hold-fast " (*n h*, fig. 1, page

7), or in the screw-chops (C). If increased power be required, the tool is pressed forward by the workman's shoulder, and when this fails to make the instrument advance, the mallet (fig. 49) must be employed to drive it into the material.

Fig. 50.

The *mortise-chisel* (fig. 50) is employed, as its name implies, for making the hole or mortise for the reception of the tenon. This tool is nearly square in section, but unlike the firmer chisel, its cutting edge is formed on a narrow instead of a wide side, to enable it to cut a contracted hole, and yet retain sufficient strength to withstand the blows of the mallet.

The *gouge* (fig. 51) acts in a similar manner to the ordinary chisels, but owing to its semi-

Fig. 51.

cylindrical shape, it is especially qualified for hollowing out deep cavities. It may, like the chisel, be driven forward by the hand when the resistance is not great. These tools are only suitable for light works, and must not be forcibly struck by the mallet; otherwise the handles may be split, as the shoulder at the root of the tang causes the wood of the handle to spread, and will eventually split it. The chisels used by carpenters are formed with sockets instead of the tangs and shoulders. The handle is fitted tightly into the socket, which effectually preserves it from splitting, notwithstanding the

Fig. 52.

violent blows which must be struck to drive the instrument into the wood when cutting the large mortises, &c., frequently required in heavy carpentry operations.

The *bevil* (fig. 52) is somewhat similar to the square (fig. 16), and differs from it only in not having a permanently fixed blade. The square, as we have before stated, can only be used for testing the truth of right-angled surfaces, which, to be correct, must form an angle of 90 degrees.

The bevil, however, can be employed for any angle by simply altering the position of the blade, which is attached to the stock by a pin that affords the requisite freedom. This tool is very useful for "trying" the truth of the mitre at the extremities of the pieces of a light frame, &c., as the kerf in the sawing-block may not be quite exact, and subsequent correction of the mitre by the plane is then necessary. The stock of the bevil must be applied to the surface of the work, and the blade to the edge or side which is to be bevilled.

The *brad-awl*, shown in two views (fig. 53), is the simplest of the boring tools for wood. It consists of a cylindrical steel wire with a chisel edge, which is formed by grinding a chamfer on two opposite sides. The awl is fixed in a small handle made of beech, box, or other hard wood. This tool answers very well for making holes in soft woods, but as it displaces rather than removes the fibre, it is apt to split hard material. The wire-worker's awl (fig. 54) is better qualified for boring hard wood, being square, and sharpened on the four corners or angles, which cut the fibre as the tool revolves. It gradually tapers also towards the extremity, which terminates in a sharp point, formed by grinding a slight chamfer for a short distance on each of the sides.

Large holes can only be made by removing the material, and much ingenuity has been displayed in the formation of "bits," which, by allowing the chips to escape while boring, save the time which would otherwise be lost in frequently withdrawing and clearing them. The simplest of these contrivances is the *shell*, also called the *gouge-bit* or *quill-bit* (fig. 55). In shape it much resembles an ordinary gouge, and

Fig. 53.   Fig. 54.   Fig. 55.

it is sharpened at the end in a similar manner. The sharp extremity shears the fibre of the wood round the margin of the hole, and the material entering the semi-cylindrical shell is removed almost as a solid piece. Holes of several inches in depth can be bored with this kind of bit, and it will work very easily if lubricated with a little tallow. When boring a deep hole, the tool is apt to go astray; it is therefore advisable to change the position of the work occasionally, to prevent the accumulation of error in one direction. If the work be turned a quarter round after every twenty revolutions of the bit, the latter will not depart far from its intended course.

A larger variety of the quill-bit is met with in the *shell-auger* (fig. 56). The body or shell still resembles a gouge, but the cutting extremity is differently formed. A plan of the cutter is shown

Fig. 56.

above. It consists of a small transverse blade, which pares away the wood, and allows it to escape into the shell.

The common gimlet (fig. 42), is a diminution of the shell-bit, with only this difference, that the former terminates in a screw instead of a sharp edge. The screw is conical in shape, gradually decreasing from the full diameter of the shell to a sharp point. The tool is drawn into the wood by the screw, and the cutting is performed by the sharp angular corner at the extremity of the fluted part. When the shell or fluted part has penetrated about an inch into the wood the instrument must be unwound to liberate the screw, and then withdrawn and emptied. The gimlet is more apt to split the wood than the gouge-bit, and should not be used near the margin of work, especially if the material be hard or brittle.

The twisted gimlet (fig. 44), to which reference has before been made, may be employed with less risk of splitting the work. The stem is conical, or larger at the upper than at the lower extremity, which is formed into a screw precisely similar to that of the fluted gimlet. Instead of a longitudinal groove or flute, a spiral groove is made in the stem for the escape of the material.

Fig. 57.

The cutting is done by the sharp extremity of the stem at the termination of the spiral groove.

The centre-bit shown in two views in fig. 57 is a very useful tool, much employed for boring holes which are required to be round, smooth, and parallel, but not very deep. The point, p, is stuck into the wood where the centre of the intended hole should exist, and after the point has penetrated a short distance, the *nicker, n,* which is sharp and knife-like, marks out the circumference of the hole. The pressure applied by the operator causes the centre-point and nicker to sink into the wood as the bit revolves, and the *cutter, c,* pares away the material within the circle described by the nicker. The efficient action of this instrument depends on the proper relative proportions and sharpness of the centre nicker and cutter. The centre must be a little longer than the nicker, to enable the tool to obtain a steady footing before it is required to withstand even the slight strain brought upon it by the nicker. The nicker must in its turn be in advance of the cutter, so that it may divide the fibre round the margin of the intended hole, previously to the removal of the wood by the cutter, which latter should have a little less radius than the nicker, as it must not touch the circumference of the hole. The nicker leads or prepares the way for the cutter throughout the entire depth of the hole, and also leaves its circumference tolerably smooth. The length of the centre from its point to the edge of the cutter is available for keeping the bit in its true position.

The bit represented in fig. 58 is unprovided with a nicker, but is furnished with two cutters, one on each side of the centre-point. If the tool be sharpened down the sides, which must also be exactly parallel, it will bore hard wood very satisfactorily in all directions of the grain.

When the bits become blunt, they can be sharpened by rubbing the cutting parts with a small slip of oilstone, which may be purchased at any tool-shop. As the grindstone cannot be employed, the bits should not be too long

Fig. 58.

neglected, otherwise it will take some time to restore them to an efficient condition. If the steel be not very hard, a fine file or a bit of gritstone may be used prior to the oilstone, if the bit has become very blunt.

The centre and small gouge-bits have motion imparted to them by the brace (fig. 59), which is simply a crank made of either iron or wood. A metal socket or *pad* is provided at the lower end, into which the shanks of the bits are inserted. The hole in the pad is square, and

Carpentry and Joinery. 127

slightly taper, and a spring catch is added to retain the bit while it is being withdrawn from the wood. The upper extremity of the brace is fitted with a swivel-cap or head, which the carpenter places against his chest when using the tool horizontally, but he holds it in his left hand when employing the instrument vertically.

Fig. 59.

The large shell-bits require much power to move them, and are therefore fitted at one end with a transverse handle, somewhat similar to that of an ordinary gimlet. Sometimes a ring or eye is formed at the extremity of the shank, and a handle is driven tightly into it.

As the amateur is not likely to require boring tools of large size, it is unnecessary to consider the formation of *twisted augurs*, &c., which are only combinations of the twisted gimlet and the centre-bit.

When using a centre-bit to bore a hole quite through a piece of work, the tool must not be allowed to pierce the opposite side, as it will leave the margin of the hole torn and uneven. Directly the centre-point appears, the bit must be withdrawn, and the work turned over. The centre-point can then be placed in the small hole it has made, and the large hole be satisfactorily finished. Very little pressure must be used, or the thin plate of wood will be forced in, and leave the edge more ragged than if the hole had been completed from one side.

CHAPTER VI.

GROOVING PLANES, ETC.

THERE are many joinery works which cannot be conveniently united by nails and screws, and even glue in some situations would be of little service. The strength and neatness of many works depend on the judicious employment of *tongued* and *grooved* attachments, *rebates, mouldings,* &c., which are formed by suitable planes, totally distinct from those used for surfacing. The surfacing-planes,

Fig. 60.   Fig. 61.

however, must in all cases be first employed to impart the requisite truth to the work, previously to applying the grooving-planes, &c.

Fig. 60 is a back, and fig. 61 a side view of

K

the *side fillister*, which is employed for planing a rebate around the edges of a panel, a portion of which is seen at A. The fillister is required to work, not only with, but also across the grain. We have seen that soft wood, like pine, cannot be smoothly planed across the grain, and that the plane must be held obliquely to enable the cutting edge of the iron to attack the fibre as favourably as possible. It must be evident that the fillister, and planes of a similar class, which are always constrained to move parallel with the edge of the work, cannot be used obliquely when cutting across the grain. To surmount this difficulty, the *iron is fixed obliquely* in the stock, instead of straight across, as in the surfacing-planes.

The depth and width of the rebate are regulated by moveable pieces attached to the stock, which are capable of great nicety of adjustment. The width is determined by the amount the loose strip or *fence, f, f,* figs. 60 or 61, is set back from the side of the stock which is towards the work, and the depth by the height the stop, *s, s,* is raised from the sole.

To make this quite clear, we will suppose that the rebate is one inch wide and one inch deep. The screws, *l, l,* which secure the fence to the sole, must be slackened, and the fence set back one inch from the side of the stock. The distance must be measured by the rule at both ends of the plane, care being taken to set the edge of the fence quite parallel to the side; the screws are then tightened. The depth is more readily adjusted, it being only necessary to raise the stop, s, s, one inch above the sole, by turning the thumb-screw, t, t, in the proper direction. Both measures are now fixed, and the iron will continue to cut until the stop, s, s, by coming in contact with the surface of the work, prevents any further encroachment. The fence, f, f, by rubbing along the edge of the work, not only determines the width of the rebate, but also keeps its shoulder parallel to the edge. It must be understood that the fence is placed against the margin of the panel from the first, and continues in contact with it until the rebate is finished.

The oblique iron, like the cutter in an ordinary surfacing-plane, is sharp only on the lower edge which works the rebate in the direction of its depth. The shoulder or perpendicular edge would therefore be left rough, if another addition were not made to the fillister. A small supplementary cutter or *scoring point*, p, p, is fixed in advance of the oblique iron, and, by dividing the fibres, makes the perpendicular edge or shoulder clean and square. The action of this little tooth or blade, seen separately on the left-hand side of fig. 60, is somewhat similar to that of the " nicker " of the centre-bit. Most of the planes for working across the grain are furnished with oblique irons and scoring-points.

The *skew rebate*, also called the *rabbet-plane*, is frequently used instead of the fillister, but owing

Fig. 62.

to the absence of the fence and stop, it is more difficult to manage satisfactorily. This tool is shown in elevation in fig. 62; fig. 63 is an end

Fig. 63.

Fig. 64.

view, and fig. 64 is a plan of the sole. The iron (fig. 65), like that on the fillister, is fixed obliquely or *askew* in the stock. No scoring-

Carpentry and Joinery. 133

point is provided, but the iron is made to act in a two-fold manner, by sharpening the right-hand edge, r, so that it may work the perpendicular side of the rebate. A hole, h, fig. 62, passes through the side of the stock to allow the shavings to escape.

Fig. 65.

Square rabbet-planes, in which the irons are set straight across the stock, are also in very general use. The iron is sharp only on the lower edge, and is employed in the lengthway of the grain. Neither the skew nor the square rabbet-plane can be used with certainty to commence a rebate, owing to the absence of a fence to determine its width or the distance from the margin of the work. A practised joiner may execute the work by the aid of a deep gauge-line, indicating the width of the rebate, and placing his fore-finger under the sole and against the margin of the board, to act as a fence. If, after gauging a deep line, the wood be roughly removed by a firmer chisel, in order to leave a shoulder to guide the plane, the difficulty will be much diminished. A narrow strip of wood is sometimes temporarily tacked on to the sole of the plane to serve as a fence, exposing only as much of the iron as the width of the intended rebate. If the perpendicular side of the rebate be left rough, the plane must be turned over to enable the iron to work it.

The *plough* (fig. 66) may be used either as a rebate or a grooving-plane, but it is more especially qualified for the latter. In some respects

Fig. 66.

the plough is similar to the fillister, being furnished with a fence and a stop. The fence, *f,* is not immediately attached to the stock, but is built on two transverse stems, *s, s,* which penetrate the sides of the stock, and afford the fence a much greater horizontal range than it could otherwise possess. The position of the fence being determined, the stems are locked by thin wedges, which are knocked in gently, so that

Carpentry and Joinery.

they may again be easily liberated. The iron is not fixed obliquely in the stock, but square across, as in the surfacing-planes. The width of the groove is the same as that of the iron, consequently the plough must be furnished with several cutters. An iron plate, *p, p,* is secured to the stock, in order to retain the cutter in the perpendicular position, which it effects by fitting into a narrow angular groove made in the back

Fig. 67.

of the latter; the plate is cut away in front of the blade to allow the shavings to escape. As the plough is almost invariably employed in the lengthway of the grain, the scoring-point is not required.

It is evident that the distance of the groove from the edge of the work against which the fence rubs, is limited to the length of the transverse stems, *s, s,* fig. 66. Frequently a groove, or perhaps several, are required much further from the margin of the work than the range of the fence will permit.

A simpler form of grooving-plane must be employed in this case, and one in which the fence forms no part of the structure.

Fig. 67 represents a grooving-plane applicable for making grooves at any distance, however remote from the edge of the work. A narrow strip of wood (*s*) or a straight edge is temporarily

Fig. 68.   Fig. 69.   F g. 70.

nailed down to guide the tool while cutting the groove. As the plane is often used across the grain, it must be furnished with a scoring-point, in fact with two—one for each side of the groove. One scoring-point will suffice if it be divided at the extremity into two teeth, as shown separately at page 129. The grooves formed by this plane are generally intended for receiving the ends of shelves; consequently their sides are the more important parts, and the bottoms may be sufficiently well worked by an iron fixed square across the stock. The stop must still be retained with the thumb-screw adjustment; or the less costly and less certain arrangement of a piece of boxwood stiffly fitted into the stock may be substituted for it.

Boards for partitions and similar works could not be properly united by simply glueing them edge to edge. The *split-deal* or *match* planes (figs. 68 and 69) are therefore used by carpenters to form the groove and tongue-joint, which is shown finished in fig. 70. These are simply grooving-planes for working with the grain: the irons are placed square in the stocks, and the scoring-points are omitted; the stops are not required, as the tool is worked until some part of the stock rests on the work. These planes are made in pairs, and must be used only for "stuff" of the thickness for which they are intended, otherwise the centre of the irons will not correspond with the centre of the work, and the groove and tongue will not be in the middle of the edge of the board.

Sometimes it is necessary to plane the perpendicular sides of grooves, &c., independently of the bottoms, to widen them sufficiently to admit a thicker shelf, &c. The rabbet and grooving-planes would be inconvenient, even if they could be used; consequently another tool, which will cut on one side only, must be employed. The *side rebate-plane* is shown in elevation in fig. 71. It will be seen, by referring to fig. 73, that the left-hand side *s* of the stock is bevilled, thus reducing the part which is the sole in other planes to a narrow edge, the sole being transferred to the side *a b;* the edge of the cutter is seen at *c*, fig. 71. The iron is

Fig. 71. Fig. 72. Fig. 73.

fixed obliquely in the stock, as may be seen at *f*, fig. 72, which is a plan of the tool. The iron is similar in shape to the stock at *s*, fig. 73, and is placed in it obliquely, to give the side edge the necessary prominence, and vertically, because the lower extremity is no longer required to operate. These planes are made in pairs, or right and left-handed, so that they may be conveniently employed in situations where the work cannot be turned round to bring the opposite edge toward the workman.

Moulding-planes are not now much employed, as mouldings can be produced by machinery at a much cheaper rate than by hand labour. The irons of moulding-planes have the exact but reversed outline of the required moulding imparted to their edges, so that the hollow or concave parts leave mouldings in relief, while the convex portions, by removing the material, make corresponding depressions.

The joiner uses moulding-planes of a simple and neat design for window-frames or *sashes*, and for the *sash-bars* between which the panes of glass are introduced. The work must be truly planed to its proper size before the moulding-plane can be employed, as this tool, like the grooving-planes, requires true surfaces to work upon.

The *sticking-board*, S S, fig. 74, is of great assistance when working, or, technically speaking, *sticking* a moulding on very slight work, like the sash-bar, b b. The sash-bar is held by jamming the tongue that is formed for holding the glass into the groove g, in the strip d d, which latter is secured to the bed S S. The moulding not being made parallel to the surface of the board, but obliquely, as may be seen by the slanting position of the plane P, the work must first be roughly bevilled by the jack-plane to lessen the labour of sticking the moulding.

The moulding-plane is provided with a fence

140   *Our Workshop.*

and a stop solid with the stock, as they do not require adjustment, as in the fillister, &c. When

Fig. 74.

the plane is applied to the work, the fence *o*, fig. 74, is placed against the edge, and is kept in contact with it until the moulding is finished.

The iron continues to remove the material till the stop *n* rests upon the surface of either the strip *d*, or the plain part of the sash-bar. On the completion of the first side, the sash-bar must be turned over and refixed. The finished side being bevilled, it cannot rest fairly on the bed, S S, therefore small wedges of wood or packing-pieces must be inserted between it and the bed to support the bar and relieve the tongue of the undue strain, which otherwise it would be required to sustain, while we were "sticking" the second side of the bar.

The tongue on the sash-bar is generally worked by a *sash-plane*, which is expressly qualified for the purpose; a fillister may, however, be employed in its absence. The moulding now in general favour for sash-bars is called the *lamb's-tongue*, which, being free from angles and sharp edges, is not disfigured by the paint which clogs and spoils the appearance of more intricate designs.

In joining, it is often necessary to stick a moulding on one side only, the other being left flat, that it may bed fairly against the panels, as in door and shutter work. The same sticking-board may be used; but as there is no tongue to the mouldings employed for door-frames, &c., the work must be fixed to the board by a thin blade of steel, called a *bench-knife*, which is driven partly into both at the back end. When several mouldings of the same pattern are required, the joiner "sticks" a long piece, which he afterwards cuts into lengths suitable for his work.

Sometimes the edges of work are rounded, or a hollow groove is formed on them in situations where a moulding is not required. The rounded or convex edge could be wrought by a surfacing-plane, but the concave or groove could not be "stuck" without a special tool. Planes called *hollows* and *rounds* are therefore used, in which the soles and irons are curved to suit the work.

Fig. 75.

These planes are made in pairs, the *round* (or convex) exactly fitting into its corresponding hollow (or concave) partner. It must be evident that the *hollow* will make the edge of the work round, and the *round* will produce a hollow or groove. A complete set comprises eighteen pairs. A good workman can sometimes make two or three sizes of hollows and rounds do duty for a moulding-plane, or he may use them to correct or otherwise modify a moulding which fails to give satisfaction.

Carpentry and Joinery. 143

Some of the principal mouldings employed in joinery are shown in fig. 75. No. 1 is simply a *rounded end,* such as would be made by a hollow plane; No. 2 is called a *quirked bead;* No. 3, *double quirk bead.* No. 4 is a *double bead and quirk;* No. 5 is a *double fillet;* No. 6 is a *torous bead;* No. 7 is an *ogee;* and No. 8 is a *reversed*

Fig. 76.

ogee; No. 9, *hollow and half-round;* No. 10 is an *ovolo and bead.* The mouldings 1 and 3 are used for projecting pieces of wood or for projecting angles; Nos. 2, 4, 5, 6 are used for horizontal joints; Nos. 7, 8, 9 are employed for capping or for bead mouldings.

The proper way of holding the moulding and

similar planes is shown in fig. 76. The back of the stock is grasped near the top by the right hand, the thumb being towards the workman, and all the fingers on the opposite side of the tool. The front end of the plane is kept well down on the work by the left thumb which is placed on the upper side of the stock. The fore-

Fig. 77.

finger, which is bent at the second joint, is pressed against the side of the stock to keep the fence in contact with the work; but the remaining fingers are closed in the palm of the hand. The plane must be lifted off the work at the termination of the strokes, as the iron will lose its keenness if drawn backwards over the work, besides subjecting the sole to useless wear.

The manner of handling the plough is represented in fig. 77. This instrument is perhaps rather difficult to hold, owing to its peculiar construction and overhanging parts. The right hand is applied to the back in a way somewhat similar to that shown in fig. 76, but the fingers are placed on the back stem to help to balance the weight of the fence. The thumb of the left hand is hooked over the forward stem : the fore and remaining fingers are then placed under its projecting end, and are allowed to rest on the fence to assist in keeping it against the work.

Our readers, unless they purpose practising on a scale almost as extensive as that of a professional joiner will not require one-half of the additional planes which we have lately brought under their notice. The amateur will probably be able to execute any groove-work he is likely to attempt by the aid of the plough, which is more generally useful than the fillister, if a choice be made between them. A good plough with eight irons may be purchased for from eighteen to twenty shillings, and a moving fillister for about eight shillings. Skew and square rebate-planes, with irons from three-quarters of an inch to two inches wide, will cost about three shillings each.

If any of the simple grooving-planes, or the

hollows and rounds and moulding planes be subsequently required, they may perhaps be procured; but unless the orders with which "Our Workshop" is favoured be very extensive, this additional stock in trade will be unnecessary.

CHAPTER VII.

MORTISING AND TENONING.

THE ordinary and simplest form of mortise and tenon is shown in fig. 79. We have already observed that the tenon must not be *less* than one-third the thickness of the scantling, or it will be weaker than the shoulders or sides of the mortise. On the other hand, the tenon must never exceed one-half the thickness of the "stuff," and this proportion can be allowed only when the mortise occurs at some distance from the ends of the material, the risk of splitting the work being then greatly diminished.

When the pieces to be united are of considerable thickness, or the scantling is square in section, it is better to make two small tenons instead of one of large size. This subdivision imparts much more stiffness to the framing, and enables it to withstand a raching or side strain much longer than it could otherwise have done. The extremity on which the tenons are to be formed, must be divided into five equal parts, and the central and two exterior portions, or *cheeks,* removed by the tenon saw, thus leaving two tenons and three shoulders, as in fig. 78. The outside " cheeks " can be separated entirely by the saw, which may be applied with equal facility to both shoulders and sides, but the shoulder or root of the central portion must be wrought by a mortising chisel, or a hole may be bored, the diameter of which must not, however,

Fig. 78.

exceed the thickness of the wood to be removed, and if the hole be made a trifle above the line of the shoulders, the square corners may afterwards be cut with a chisel.

The practical application of mortising and tenoning may be better understood if we consider the construction of a simple rectangular frame such as fig. 79. The long pieces, A B, C D, are called the *styles,* and the cross bars, A C, B D, which are usually shorter, are named the *rails.* No invariable rule can be given for the proportions of the several parts of the framing, as its strength must be regulated in a great measure by the character of the work, and the purpose

Carpentry and Joinery. 149

for which it is intended. In joining, the styles and rails vary from about one-fourth to one-fifth of the internal width of the frame; but in cabinet-making, less strength being required, one-sixth

Fig. 79.

is the most usual proportion. The thickness of a style varies from one-third to one-half of its width, but the joiner is guided more by the size of the work, the nature of the material, and his own experience, than by any actual rule.

Having determined upon the size of the frame and the material of which to construct it, the styles and rails must next be cut out with the hand-saw, being careful to allow something for planing up, and also a little excess in the length of the pieces for trimming off after the frame is united. If the frame be small, the "stuff" should be planed up as one piece, and afterwards cut into the required lengths. Sometimes it may be difficult to procure wood long enough to do this; but perhaps two pieces can be found from which either a pair of styles or a pair of rails may be cut, or one style and rail from each piece. Before cutting off the lengths, one side of the stuff must be marked by a pencil from end to end, to enable us to distinguish it from the other after the wood has been divided.

The internal dimensions of the frame must be marked on each of the four portions, the length on the styles and the width on the rails. Great care must be taken to make the lines correspond exactly on the respective pieces, as any want of truth will mislead us when cutting the mortises and tenons; the frame, also, when put together, would be crooked. This contingency may be avoided by laying the styles side by side on the bench, and scribing the lines across them both with a square and scriber. The lines should be equidistant from the ends of the styles, as both extremities require a little allowance for finally trimming off. The length of the frame being thus marked on one side, the styles must be taken separately, and marked on the remaining sides, or all round, by the aid of the square and

Fig. 80.

scriber. The rails must be subjected to similar treatment.

The mortises and tenons must now be marked out and worked. Fig. 80 is an enlarged view of the mortise and tenon, the former being made in the style S, while the latter is formed on the rail

R. The thickness of the tenon should not exceed one-third of that of the rail; but a little latitude may be allowed in this, and the mortise-chisel which is nearest to the required thickness may be selected.

The *mortise-gauge* (fig. 81) is provided with two points, which may be adjusted to the required width of the mortise. The chisel chosen for the work may be lightly stuck into

Fig. 81.

the edges of the styles and rails to mark its own thickness, to which the gauge can be then readily set. The common marking-gauge may be employed, but it must be adjusted twice, as the gauge must be applied only to the "face" side of the work, which was marked previously to cutting off the four pieces. These lines, shown at l, l, fig. 80, must be marked on both the edges and across the ends of the four members of the frame.

It is evident that the tenons must be narrower than the rails, otherwise they would break through the extremities of the styles when the ends of the latter are trimmed off. By inspecting fig. 80 it will be seen that the tenon t is cut back from both the edges of the rail R, but much more from the *outer* than from the inner edge. It is not, however, cut off close to the shoulder on the outer edge, but is allowed to stand up about half an inch, as shown at S. The amount, however, is regulated by the size of the work or some peculiarity in it.

The tenon is not necessarily cut back from the inside, unless a groove for a panel is made in the inner edges of the styles and rails. In this case the inner edge of the tenon is made level with the bottom of the groove, the depth of which latter may also determine the projection of the part S from the shoulder.

If the frame is not to be fitted with a panel, the groove will probably not be required, and the *inner* edges of the tenons may be made level with the inside edges of the rails. The lines which were scribed on the styles to indicate the internal length of the frame will also serve to mark the inner ends of the mortises, the outer ends being marked by similar lines, which are made as much beyond the first as the width of the intended tenons. If a groove be necessary, the lines determining the length of the styles will not be correct for the inner ends of the mortise; consequently new lines must be marked in advance, the intervening space being equal to the depth of the groove.

The frame represented in figs. 79 and 80 is furnished with a panel, and the groove to receive it is shown by the dotted lines g, g, in fig. 79. The width of the the tenons, which varies from about one-half to two-thirds that of the rail, being determined upon, it is now necessary to mark out the mortises in the manner already described, and at once proceed to form these parts and put the frame together.

In joining, the styles being generally light, they are placed side by side on the bench, with their inner edges upwards, and are held by the holdfast; but if the work be heavy, as in carpentry, it must be laid on the mortising-stool, and the operator sits upon it. If the mortise be unusually wide or deep, the greater portion of the wood may be removed by a gouge-bit or centre-bit, and the mortise is afterwards finished by an ordinary chisel.

The chisel is held in the left, and a mallet of proportionate size in the right hand. The chisel is mostly held with its face towards the workman, and the first incision is made about one-sixth from the end of the mortise, care being taken to keep the edge of the tool exactly square, and within the gauge lines. After a few moderate blows of the mallet, the chisel should be shaken backwards and forwards to liberate it, and another cut is then made a little in advance of the first, the chisel being slightly inclined instead of perpendicular. If the inclination be sufficient the second cut will join the first at the bottom, and by thrusting the handle of the chisel from him, the workman is enabled to prise up and remove the small wedge-shaped core, which is the result of the two cuts. The chamfer, or bevil of the chisel, is used as the fulcrum, and it acts against the solid wood behind it. When cutting the ends of the mortise, the chisel must be held perpendicularly, and the handle is moved towards the centre of the mortise, to displace the chips, the edge of the tool being the fulcrum in this case. When prising up the chips the chisel must never be allowed to press against the angles or edges of the mortise, or they will thereby be bruised and disfigured.

Having cut the mortise about half-way through, the style must be turned over and finished from the opposite side. Provided the chisel is kept parallel to the sides of the work and strictly within the gauge lines, no great difficulty will be experienced in cutting the mortise true. If the excavations do not exactly meet, in consequence of the chisel going astray, the irregularities must be cut away by a firmer-chisel. A good workman will "drive" a mortise so accurately as to render any subsequent correction unnecessary.

The ends of the mortise are bevilled from the outer edge to the centre, to make room for the wedges by which the tenon will be fixed in the mortise.

Having driven all the mortises, the tenons must be marked from them and cut out. If proper care has been bestowed in cutting the mortises, the gauge lines will be still visible, and it would be only necessary to cut the tenons to the lines which have already been gauged on the rails, to ensure a good fit. As a precautionary measure, however, and one which the amateur ought never to neglect, the styles and rails should be allowed to lie on the bench, their "face" sides upwards, and the ends of the rails must be placed in contact with the inner edges of the styles, and the tenons marked from their corresponding mortises. The pieces should be numbered in the order in which they are marked, to avoid misplacement when fitting the frame together. If the original gauge lines on the rails be found to tally with the mortises, the work is accurate, and we may proceed to cut the tenons;

but if there be any discrepancy, new lines must be gauged, and distinguished by short pencil-marks, as the false lines might lead us astray. The lines which were marked on the rails to indicate the internal width of the frame are also correct for the shoulders of the tenons.

One of the rails must now be fixed perpendicularly in the screw-chops, the shoulders of the intended tenon being just above the surface of the bench. Either the tenon or the sash-saw may be used to cut down the sides of the tenon, and the greatest care must be taken to keep the instrument accurately to the gauge lines, which must not be obliterated, but should be visible to the last. Having cut down both sides of the tenon, the rail must be removed from the chops and laid on the bench, and the transverses, or shoulder-cuts, must be made by either the dovetail or the carcass saw. It is immaterial whether the sides or shoulders be first wrought, but the saw must never be permitted to penetrate beyond the lines, or the strength of the tenon will be much impaired.

If the tenon has been properly cut by the saw, it will require no further finish, and the chisel should be used only to clean out the angles between the shoulders and the sides, and perhaps to reduce the thickness and width of the extremity of the tenon, to enable it to enter the mortise. If, however, a few light blows of the mallet fail to send the tenon home, it must be withdrawn, and those parts which show signs of having bound, must be pared down by an ordinary chisel, the flat side of which is applied to the work. Very little should be removed at a time, and only in exceedingly thin shavings. The parts must be again put together, and if still too tight, again separated and "eased." The grooves for the panel must be ploughed in the inner edges of the styles and rails, after the mortises and tenons are finished.

The necessity for true and careful workmanship will be fully admitted when the four members of the frame are attached. If either a tenon or a mortise be, even in the slightest degree, out of square, the frame will be crooked, and the fault can be rectified only by paring a little off the opposite sides of the faulty tenon, close to the shoulder on one side, and near the extremity on the other. If the parts be much out of truth, this treatment will fail to effect a cure, as the tenon would be made so loose in the mortise that the joint would be practically worthless.

If the work prove satisfactory, the wedges for fixing the tenons may now be cut out and temporarily fitted. The wedges must be bevilled on one side only, and to the same angle as the outer ends of the mortises.

within the mortises, and the blows should be distributed evenly to both ends, in order to drive the style straight. If the material of which the frame is constructed be soft and easily bruised, a small piece of wood should be interposed, to shield it from the strokes of the mallet. The ordinary hammer may then be used without fear of damaging the work.

When the glue has become thoroughly hard, the extremities of the tenons and styles must be trimmed off, as shown at C D, fig. 79. This should be done by one of the back saws, care being taken not to cut either the style or rails, which would be thereby much disfigured.

In joinery, the panel P, fig. 82, fits into grooves in the styles and rails, as shown at S;

Fig. 82.

but in cabinet-making a rebate is generally made, as seen at S', and the panel is secured by slips of wood which are glued on to the frame after it is finished. In joinery, a moulding (*m*) is glued to the inner edges of the frame, to impart a finished appearance to the work. The moulding must not be glued to the panel, as the shrinking of the latter will separate the former from the frame.

Sometimes it is necessary to make the panel flush with one side of the frame, as in fig. 83. The styles and rails are grooved in the usual manner; but the panel P is made thicker, and a rebate is formed around its edges, in order to make a tongue to fit into the groove.

Fig. 83.

Occasionally, neither grooves nor rebates are employed; and the panel is retained by the slip on one side, and by a light moulding on the other. In this case the moulding must be rebated on one edge, so that it may rest partly on the surface of the styles and rails and partly against their inner edges. This plan is generally adopted only in cabinet work when the inner edges of the rails are curved instead of straight. The curved mouldings cannot be wrought by a plane, therefore they must be carved by hand.

Sometimes in cabinet-making and light joinery, the mortises do not extend quite through the styles, and as the tenons cannot then be wedged up, the strength of the work in a great measure depends upon the accuracy and close-fitting of the parts.

When the rails are so wide that the width of the tenons would exceed four times their thickness, it is advisable to divide the tenons into two or more parts, as shown in fig. 84, which represents a wide rail having two tenons with three shoulders, which latter enter the groove in the styles. This kind of rail is unsuitable for the ends of a frame, the tenons being too near its edges; but it is used intermediately when the

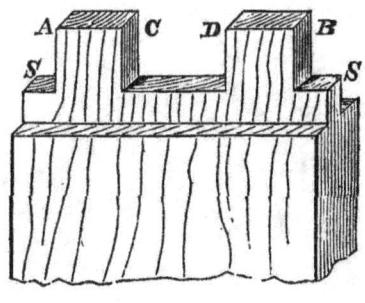

Fig. 84.

styles are long, and require additional support, or when several panels are to be introduced.

As a general rule, the space C D between the tenons should not be less than one-third the width of the original single tenon A B, and the shoulders, S, S, vary from one-third to one-half the width of one of the tenons.

In fig. 85 is shown the formation of the tenons and mortises for a wide external rail. The construction is very similar to that represented in fig. 80, and the only important difference is the subdivision of the tenon into two parts the object being to strengthen the style by leaving a central division in the mortise.

Another method of mortising and tenoning is represented in fig. 86. A single tenon, about

Fig. 85.

two-thirds the width of the rail, is formed at the extremity of the latter, and two feather-slips (*f, f*) are let into the shoulders of the tenon. Corresponding grooves (*g, g*), to receive the feathers are ploughed in the styles on each side of the mortise.

Before using the plough, the inner ends (i, i) of the grooves must be cut with a small mortise-chisel of the same width as the plough-iron, to enable the chips to detach themselves. A hole of the same diameter as the width of the intended

Fig. 86.

groove may be first made; the chisel can then be used with greater facility.

The feathers are useful, inasmuch as they impart greater steadiness to the frame by checking any tendency of the shoulders to rock on the style.

CHAPTER VIII.

DOVETAILING.

A BOX which is either simply glued or nailed together, can be considered only as a very rough specimen of joinery. If however, the sides be dovetailed together, and the work be neatly executed, it will present a finished and artistic appearance.

Small boxes and similar light works which do not require much strength are frequently *mitred*

Fig. 87.

and *keyed*: this mode of attachment is shown in fig. 87. The extremities of the end and side pieces of the box are mitred or planed to an angle of 45 degrees on the shooting-board (fig. 22, page 49). If this be properly done, the ends will form angles of 90 degrees with the sides, and the work will be truly square. The four pieces must be glued together in the ordinary manner, and when the glue is quite hard, several cuts, inclining alternately a few degrees upwards and downwards, must be made by a back saw across each of the corners of the box;

Fig. 88.

small pieces of veneer or other thin wood, K K, called *keys*, must then be glued and pressed into the saw kerfs. This joint is very easily made, and is stronger than many people imagine. It often proves a useful substitute for the dovetail, especially in light articles, such as work-boxes, &c., which are usually veneered.

The simplest form of dovetail attachment is shown complete in No. 88. In fig. 89 the two pieces which respectively represent the side and end of a box are detached, in order to exhibit the formation of the joint.

The four pieces which are to form the sides and ends of the box must be cut out a trifle longer than they will ultimately be required, to

Fig. 89.

allow for trimming off after the work is put together. The end pieces must be as long or wide as the external width of the box, in order that the dovetail pins which are to be made on them may penetrate the sides.

The internal length and width of the box must be marked on the sides and ends respectively, care being taken to make the lines equi-distant from the extremities of the "stuff." The marking-gauge may be set to one of the lines, and the four pieces can then be gauged at each end and on both sides, or the square and scriber may be employed. These lines, which also determine the bottoms of the pins and dovetails, are seen at *g, g,* fig. 89.

Sometimes the pins on the piece P are the same size as the dovetails on D, which latter occupy the spaces between the pins; but in joinery and cabinet-work the pins are made only one-fourth or one-fifth the size of the dovetails. The strength of the work is thus diminished, but greater neatness is secured, as less of the cross-grain of the end pieces is seen on the sides of the box, which are generally more exposed to view than the ends.

The pins must be marked by a pencil on the two end pieces of a box, care being taken to have equal spaces between them. A practised workman can set out the pins unaided by either rule or compasses; but the amateur would be unwise, while yet inexperienced, to work without their assistance. The pins should be marked not only on the extremities, but also on the sides of the end pieces, to afford some guide in sawing the sides of the pins straight. The pins must be about as wide again on the inner as on the outer side of the box, and the two external pins should be at least twice as large as the others. In fig. 89 the dovetails, *d, d,* are external, consequently all the pins are of uniform size.

Having set out the pins at both extremities of the end pieces, one of these latter must be fixed perpendicularly in the chops of the bench. Both sides of each of the pins must be very carefully sawn down to the guage line *g, g,* by the dovetail saw. The lines representing the pins should almost be left standing in their favour, the waste of the saw being taken from the spaces. If the material be thick and the spaces wide, the wood between the pins may be cut out by the turning or frame-saw, fig. 47; the bottoms and the angles at the roots of the pins can afterwards be pared out by the firmer-chisel.

In light joinery or cabinet-work, however, the sides of the pins are always cut by the dovetail saw, and the wood between them removed by the chisel. To accomplish this, the end must be removed from the chops and laid on the bench, and, if necessary, fixed by the holdfast. The chisel must be sufficiently narrow to pass easily between the pins, and it should be applied to the work about the sixteenth of an inch outside the gauge-line. The tool is driven into the wood by a few blows of a light mallet, and after taking several slanting cuts, the work is turned over and completed from the opposite side.

The bottoms must next be finished, the gauge-lines being very cautiously approached. In taking the final cuts, the chisel must be allowed slightly to overhang the ends of the pins, in order to undercut the bottoms, to make them hollow or lower in the centre, instead of quite flat. As the cuts are taken half through from the opposite sides of the work, and meet in the centre, there is no difficulty in making the middle lower, and close contact of the edges with the side pieces will be insured.

Having finished all the pins, the dovetail must next be *marked from them* and wrought. One of the sides is laid on the bench, and upon it one of the ends is placed in its intended position. The extremities of the pins rest on the surface of the side piece, and their wide faces must be set upon the gauge-line which represents the bottoms of the dovetails.

The end being properly adjusted in every direction, a scriber is passed along the sloping sides of the pins, in order to mark their exact shape on the side piece. The spaces just marked for the reception of the pins are generally too contracted to be cut out by the turning saw, and are therefore usually wrought by a dovetail saw, and an ordinary chisel applied in the manner already described.

If the spaces between the dovetails be carefully

removed without entirely obliterating the marks which were made by the scriber, the pins and dovetails will be a little too large, and by slightly compressing each other when the work is united, a close and firm joint is insured. Leaving the parts a trifle too large will not remedy any defect in the workmanship, and if much be allowed for compression, the wood will probably split before the pins are driven home.

The three remaining extremities or corners of the side pieces are marked from their corresponding pins, and wrought in the same manner as the first corner just completed.

When the amateur has become tolerably expert he will find it quite as easy to follow some established routine as to conduct the work irregularly. The pins, therefore, should be marked out on both the extremities of the end pieces, and then wrought by the saw and the chisel. When using the chisel, one piece may be laid on the other, the end of the upper piece being set back, so as not to cover the guage-line of its neighbour; both are then fixed by the holdfast. The extremity of each piece being towards the workman, he can use his chisel advantageously; when both pieces have been cut half through, they are turned over and finished from the other side. The opposite extremities are then placed in front, and wrought in the same manner. All the dovetails are next marked from the pins, and the ends and sides must be numbered in the order in which they are scribed. The sides are then fixed and wrought like the ends.

The pins and dovetails must not be made with any considerable angle or bevel, or the connection will be deficient in strength. More bevel, however, may be allowed if hard wood, such as oak or mahogany, be employed, but in deal and other soft or brittle materials, the parts should be only slightly bevilled.

We will now proceed to glue the box together. One of the ends must be fixed vertically in the screw-chops, the pins of one extremity being a little above the level of the bench. The pins and bottoms must be sparingly covered with thin glue; the first side is then held horizontally, and the pins are directed into their corresponding sockets between the dovetails. A small piece of wood which is smooth on the underside must be laid on the dovetails, to save them from being bruised by the hammer which is now used to drive the dovetails home to the bottoms or shoulders of the pins. As the length of the pins exceeds the thickness of the side, the hammer-block must be set back when they become level with the surface, to allow them to rise to their full extent. The first end is now released, the second being fixed in its stead, and the process just described is repeated. Three sides of the square having been united, the work must be removed from the chops and laid on the bench preparatory to attaching the fourth side, which will complete the square and form the carcase.

The first side is now supported upon two strips of wood of equal thickness, which are placed one under each extremity, and just within the projecting ends of the pins, in order to keep them clear of the bench, and afford the work a steady base. The pins corresponding to the dovetails of the second side are next glued; the side is carefully adjusted, so that all the pins may fairly enter into their respective sockets, and is then driven home. The hammer and block are used at each end alternately, and at short intervals, in order to drive the side down as evenly as possible.

Although this form of dovetail, if well made, is a neat and useful joint for plain works, it is not suitable for cabinet-work and fancy articles unless the end grain of the pins and dovetails is hidden by veneer. Small boxes, writing desks, &c., are generally made of mahogany, rosewood, or some other ornamental wood; and as veneer is not then employed, the joint must be so formed that the end wood may be concealed.

The *lap-dovetail*, which is seen complete in fig. 92, is used for the description of work last named. Fig. 91 represents the formation of this attachment. The end grain of the pins and dovetails is effectually enclosed, but a narrow strip of the cross-grain end of the piece, P, is observable at E: this, however, is disguised by rounding the corner after the work is put together. The gauge-lines g, g, which denote how

Fig. 90.

far the pins and dovetails must extend inwards, are marked as in fig. 89. It will be seen, by inspecting fig. 91, that neither the pins nor the dovetails extend quite through the wood in which they are respectively formed; hence the concealment of their end grain; and it is immaterial in which piece the pins or the dovetails are made. The depth of the dovetails is generallly about one-eighth inch less than the thickness of the piece containing them, and the pins are of corresponding length. If the ends of the pins were made level with the end of the piece P, in which they are cut, the pins would reach the bottoms of the dovetails before the piece P had entirely covered the end wood of D, and the bottoms of the dovetails would remain in sight. A hollow angular corner would result, and a

Fig. 91.

strip of wood called a *corner line*, must be glued into it to finish the joint; this is sometimes called a *secret dovetail*. In the "lap dovetail," however, the pins are set back one-eighth inch from the end E, of the side P, or the amount the dovetails are shallower than the thickness of the piece D. By this means the depth l, l, of the lap is made to equal or slightly exceed the thickness of the piece D, consequently the end of D is covered by it, as seen in fig. 92.

Sometimes the lap is not formed on the piece containing the pins as in fig. 91, and the extremities of the pins are then level or flush with the end E. In this case the lap must be worked in the piece in which the dovetails are cut.

Fig. 92.

Before the sides and ends are cut to their lengths, the workman must decide in which pair he will form the laps, as this pair must be cut to the external dimensions of the work, but the other pair being placed between the laps, the thickness of the latter must be deducted.

The *half-lap dovetail* is a modification of the last-named, and is much used for the fronts of drawers. The pins are cut in the front piece, represented by P, fig. 91, but their extremities are level with the end E. The dovetails are cut quite through the side pieces, which are only about half the thickness of the front. If the front is to be veneered, the dovetails are made as in figs. 88 and 89.

The *mitre dovetail,* figs. 92 and 93, is the neatest and most difficult to make of the group. The

Fig. 93.

four pieces must be cut to the external dimensions of the work, and then rebated at each end. This rebate should be about an eighth of an inch square, and similar to the lap E, in the piece P, fig. 91, in which E is about an eighth of an inch thick, and projects the same amount beyond the ends of the pins. After cutting and fitting the pins and dovetails, the rebates or laps must be mitred by a rebate plane. The bevel (fig. 52, page 120), if set to an angle of 45 degrees, will greatly facilitate the process. When finished, no portion of the end grain is seen, and the box has the appearance of being simply mitred.

When the pins and dovetails do not extend quite through the work, the saw can only be applied obliquely, and not to the full depth; the work is then completed by the chisel.

If the cover of a box consist simply of a flat piece, like the bottom, it is apt to warp, and will not then fit closely. When the cover is formed with a dovetailed rim, it has the appearance of a shallow box or tray, and the box to which it is attached is said to have a *tea-chest top*. If the box and its cover were made separately, it would be difficult to ensure their exact agreement, and the labour of dovetailing, &c., would also be increased.

The required truth may be obtained by constructing the box and cover as one piece, and dividing them afterwards by the saw. The four pieces, which must be wide or deep enough to form the box and its cover, are dovetailed together in either of the ways already described. On adding the two pieces which respectively represent the top and bottom of the box, the work resembles a square block, or a cube, if all the sides be equal. These pieces may be simply glued upon the edges of the box, although the neater and most usual way is to rebate the four sides and the top in order to allow the latter to sink, so that less than half its actual thickness is seen. If the box be constructed with a mitre dovetail, and the top and bottom be rebated and mitred, no end wood will be visible, as all the joints occur on the angles of the work. This is the neatest method of attaching the six pieces, but as the workmanship must be exceedingly good, it is seldom employed, and then only in works of the best quality.

Whenever the box and cover are made together, one of the dovetail pins in each of the side and end pieces must occur on the line of division. This line, which represents the depth of the cover, must be gauged all round on the outside, and should fall exactly on the centre of the pins, which must be at least as large again as the others, so that when cut in half they may equal them in size. The joint pins and dovetails must be pared away to a mitre, for if they be left square like the others, rectangular lines will be seen on cutting open the carcase—that is, separating the cover and box by the carcase saw.

CHAPTER IX.

VENEERING.

OUR readers already know that veneering is the art of glueing a very thin sheet of valuable wood upon a thick piece of a cheaper description.

Veneer is laid either with a caul or the veneering hammer. The former is always required for curved work, of which it must be an exact counterpart; it may also, when flat, be employed for plain surfaces; the veneering hammer, however, can be used only for flat work.

The surface of the work, and both sides of the veneer, must be roughened all over by the *toothing-plane*, which is fitted with a perpendicular iron, the edge of which is serrated like an exceedingly fine saw. The small grooves made by this tool are technically called *keys* or *teeth*, and afford the glue a much firmer hold than it could otherwise possess.

If the veneer is to be laid by a caul, this latter must now be prepared, and should be fully as large as the work, and several pair of screw-clamps must also be selected. Each pair of clamps consists of two strong bars of wood, connected at the ends by screw-bolts and nuts. The inner edges of the bars should be slightly convex, or rounding in the direction of their length, so that they may touch the middle of the caul and under side of the work earlier than the outer edges or margin. The bars must be adjusted to the proper distance apart, so that the caul and work may just slip between them, for if too much be left to screw up after laying the veneer, the glue will lose its fluidity before the pressure is applied, and the work may be unsound in consequence.

We will now proceed to lay a piece of veneer with a flat caul. The caul must be placed near the fire so that it may be made thoroughly hot, care, however, being taken not to scorch it; and the sides should be frequently changed to equalize the influence of the heat, which may otherwise distort the surface. The upper surface of the work, and both sides of the veneer having been toothed, they are next made very warm, and the surface of the work is brushed over quickly with very thin glue or size; the veneer is then glued and laid on the work, being hastily rubbed down by the outstretched hands of two or three workmen; the hot caul is then placed on the veneer, and the clamps are slipped on and screwed down at intervals of two or three inches. The heat of the caul quickly penetrates the thin veneer, making the glue exceedingly fluid, and the pressure supplied by the clamps soon expels the greater portion of it, and causes the veneer to bed very closely to the work. The clamps must be screwed down as evenly as possible, so that the surplus glue may escape freely from the centre of the work. This may generally be ensured by screwing down both ends of the clamps equally, so that the bars, which are slightly rounding or convex, may touch the centre of the work first, gradually yielding as the pressure increases, until they bear throughout.

The same method is pursued when laying veneer upon curved works, but the face of the caul, as before observed, must be an exact counterpart of the surface to be veneered. The clamps must not be removed until the work is quite cold; or for about twelve hours. The glue is not considered to be thoroughly hard under two or three days, and if it be disturbed before it is quite dry, the soundness of the work is endangered. Sometimes the work is laid on the floor, the veneer downwards, and is then covered with shavings, which exclude the air, and cause the drying to proceed more gradually.

The amateur will seldom, if ever, have occasion to veneer curved works, and will not, therefore, require apparatus such as clamps and cauls. The veneering hammer is the only tool required for laying veneer on flat surfaces. This hammer, which has a very wide and thin pane, may be purchased for about two shillings or half a crown. Sometimes the workman prefers to make the hammer himself. As this is not difficult of accomplishment, some of our readers may desire to do the same. The hammer head in this case is made of a block of hard wood, about three or four inches square, and a round handle is inserted in the centre. One of the sides is next sawn down about an inch, and a piece of sheet iron or steel, say an eighth of an inch thick, is tightly fitted into the kerf, and should project about one quarter of an inch. The edge of the sheet metal or pane must be rounded with a file and made quite smooth, so that it may not injure the surface of the veneer. The opposite side to that in which the pane is fitted should be rounded so that it may not hurt the workman's hand, as he will be obliged to press heavily on the head to make the hammer act efficiently.

Everything being in readiness, the surface of the work, which has been made as hot as prudence will permit, is hastily covered with very fluid glue, which should also be as hot as the water bath can make it. The veneer must next be brushed over with glue on the side which is to be laid on the work, and just before laying, it should be held before a fire of shavings to render the glue perfectly fluid, as it soon loses its heat, however expeditiously the operation may be performed. After turning the veneer down upon the work, it must be rubbed over with the outstretched hands of two or three people, the pressure being first applied at the centre and gradually extended towards the margin. The upper side of the veneer is now washed over with hot size, which serves the double purpose of imparting fresh heat to the rapidly-cooling glue, and lessening the friction of the veneering hammer, which we are now about to use.

One man would scarcely be able to lay a piece of veneer satisfactorily; and as the soundness of the work in a great measure depends upon the despatch with which it is conducted, as many hands as can be spared, or as can conveniently assist, generally lend their aid.

The pane of the hammer is applied at the middle of the work; the operator bears heavily on the head, and slowly wriggles the tool by its handle towards the margin. He again returns to the centre, and works down a line a little to one side of the former course, and so on repeatedly, until the entire surface has been traversed.

During the operation the surface of the veneer must be frequently washed over with hot size, to lessen the friction of the hammer, and to supply fresh heat to the glue. Inattention to this precaution would probably result in the destruction of the veneer. The pressure applied to the narrow edge of the pane is apt to cause it to tear the veneer if the latter become nearly dry. The heat and moisture supplied by the size tend to make the veneer pliable, and greatly facilitate the escape of the glue, which accumulates in advance of the pane in its progress from the centre of the work to the margin, where it is discharged. The solidity of the work may generally be tested by tapping the surface all over with the back of the hammer; and if some of the blows produce a dull hollow sound, the veneer is not in actual contact at those parts with the foundation or work. The pane must again be applied to the faulty spots, and if the glue be too far set to yield, the inner vessel of the glue-pot may be placed thereon, to furnish the necessary warmth. The difficulty of the process materially increases with the magnitude of the work, and soundness is more uncertain than when cauls and clamps are employed. The hammer is very useful for laying narrow strips or for small works that can be quickly completed, and in such cases is generally used, although the before-named apparatus may be at hand.

If veneered works when in use be placed too

close to the fire, the veneer is apt to become blistered, and it is impossible to rectify the mischief except by re-laying. To remove the veneer, the surface must be washed with boiling water, and then wiped with a coarse cloth, to remove any dirt or grease that may adhere to it. The article must next be placed with the veneer towards the fire, or a hot caul may be placed upon it. When thoroughly hot, the surface must be rubbed over with linseed oil, and again exposed to the fire, or supplied with a fresh caul. The oil will soon sink through the veneer, and soften the glue, when the edges of the veneer may be gently raised by a chisel, being very careful not to split it. The heat and application of oil must be continued until the veneer is entirely separated from the foundation.

Before attempting to re-lay the veneer, all the old glue must be scraped off, after which either of the processes we have described may be adopted.

CHAPTER X.

VARNISHING AND FRENCH POLISHING.

THE beauty of the handsomely-figured woods is greatly enhanced by polishing, and the surface of the work is also less likely to be affected by moisture. Pine and other soft woods which are frequently stained in imitation of the more showy varieties, are generally varnished. Carved works which are at all intricate are almost invariably varnished.

The surface of the work must be very carefully finished, previous to the application of either varnish or French polish. Clean and straight-grained woods can be planed so smooth that the application of fine glass-paper will impart the requisite finish. Some of the ornamental woods cannot be smoothly planed, owing to their cross-grained nature, the surface must therefore be completed by scraping with a steel scraper, and rubbing it with glass-paper. Any imperfections in the surface, such as cavities left by knots which have fallen out, or slight flaws, must be filled with stopping, which must not, however, contain any oil or grease; some of the gums, or wax, coloured to resemble the work, should be employed.

The varnish may be placed in an ordinary preserve-jar, across the mouth of which a string or wire should be stretched, for wiping the brush upon every time it is dipped, as much waste is occasioned by pressing the brush against the edge of the jar, when we wish to remove the surplus varnish. Sufficient varnish should be poured into the jar to cover the hairs of the brush, which will thereby be kept soft and in good working order. When not in use, the jar must be closely covered to hinder the evaporation of the spirit, otherwise the varnish will become too thick; and if dust be not carefully excluded, the varnish will be spoilt. If the varnish become too thick, its fluidity may be restored by adding a small quantity of spirits of wine. Turpentine and oil varnishes must be thinned by their respective solvents.

Spirit varnishes are generally applied with a camel's hair brush, which must of course vary in size according to the magnitude of the work. When the surfaces are extensive, large flat camel's-hair brushes are used; but they are so thin in proportion to their width, that they cannot hold much varnish, and require to be frequently re-filled when working on a large surface, whereby the difficulty of laying a smooth coat is greatly increased. It is advisable under these circumstances to dilute the varnish with a little spirits of wine, which will make it flow more readily, and prevent it drying too rapidly. Turpentine and oil varnishes are applied with brushes formed of very fine and soft bristles, and sometimes ordinary oil colour-brushes are employed; but these latter are generally too harsh, and the adhesion of the varnish is apt to draw out the hairs, which are not so well secured as in proper varnishing brushes.

Whether the varnishes be spirit, turpentine, or oil, they must be so fluid, that they will spread or flow evenly over the entire surface. It is far better to apply several thin coats than to lay on one or two of greater thickness; and in the latter case it would be almost, if not quite, impossible to obtain a smooth, regular surface.

The varnish is apt to accumulate at the edges of the work, and to lie too thickly in any angles or mouldings with which it may be ornamented. To avoid this, the varnish must be first applied at a little distance from the edge, which may be subsequently coated when the brush is nearly empty. The brush must be used from end to end of the work, the strokes being rapid and light, at the same time taking care to work out any air-bubbles that may form. If the surface be small, very little difficulty will be experienced, as the brush can be passed over it at one stroke, and if this stroke appear imperfect, a second stroke may be made at right angles to the first, and, if necessary, a third may be made in the same direction as the first. This must be quickly done, otherwise the varnish will begin to set, and streaky lines will be left on the surface. If any of the hairs of the brush become detached. and stick on the varnished surface, they must be immediately removed before the varnish hardens. If this be neglected until the varnish is dry, the hairs or other extraneous matter must be carefully picked out with the point of a pen-knife, and the surface must then be rubbed level with fine glass-paper prior to the next coat.

Varnishing should be conducted in a warm and thoroughly dry atmosphere, and the work must be allowed to acquire the same temperature as the apartment before commencing operations. This is specially important when using spirit varnishes, which are exceedingly susceptible to moisture, and cold currents of air or draughts, which will chill the varnish and deprive it of its brightness. The presence of invisible moisture or vapour in the atmosphere is soon made apparent by the milky, opaque appearance it imparts to the varnish. The brightness of the chilled coat may sometimes be restored by quickly and lightly applying another coat before the former becomes set, having taken necessary precautions to prevent a recurrence of the previous failure. The newly-varnished surface should then be held at a moderate distance from the fire, in order to liquify the chilled surface and restore its brilliancy. Great care must be taken not to place the work too close to the fire, as the varnish is very easily blistered: should this occur, the only remedy is to clean off the varnish with glass-paper, and recommence the operation.

The difficulty of laying an even coat of varnish is greatly increased when the surface to be covered is extensive. It is generally advisable to use the brush from one edge to the other in the narrowest direction. If the surface be too wide to admit of this course, the varnish must be laid in separate portions, thinning off the edges of each portion with the brush, in order that they may overlap each other, and so disguise the joint.

Each coat of varnish must be allowed to become thoroughly hard before applying the next, as the latest coat shields the one below it from the air, and prevents it drying properly. The successive coats must be laid as expeditiously as possible, as the fresh varnish is very liable to soften that which has been previously applied, if the brush be passed frequently over it, and to occasion an irregular chilled appearance in the new surface. It may be observed, that if a surface present any inequalities, it must be rubbed over with fine glass-paper before laying the next coat. As a general rule, spirit varnishes require from three to four hours for drying between each coat; turpentine varnishes about ten or twelve hours; and oil varnishes at least twenty-four hours. The time allowed for drying must in some measure be regulated by the state of the atmosphere, and the quantity of spirit, turpentine, or oil contained in the varnish. The hardness of the varnish may be tested by pressing the knuckles on the surface; if no mark be left, the varnish is quite dry and in a fit state to receive a fresh coat.

If the work is required to be very highly finished, the varnish may be polished when the last coat has become thoroughly hard. It is presumed that the surface is free from brush-marks, or other blemishes, before any attempt is made at polishing, which otherwise would be so much labour wasted.

Mix about two ounces of finely-powdered tripoli with water to the consistency of thick cream; apply a small quantity to a piece of fine flannel which has been folded four times, and rub the surface of the work with moderate pressure. Care must be taken to keep the surface wet during the process. The progress of the polishing may always be ascertained by wiping a small portion of the work with a sponge, and when the surface has an even gloss, the tripoli may be wiped off, and the work dried with a clean washleather. A little fine tallow or mutton-suet must now be taken on the finger, with which the surface must be touched in several places. The surface is then rubbed with the fingers or the palm of the hand; clean wheat-flour is next dusted over the work, and is also rubbed with the fingers; after the removal of the flour, the surface should be gently rubbed with an old silk handkerchief, which will impart a brilliant lustre to the varnish.

French polish is a varnish or lacker, which is not, however, applied with a brush, like ordinary varnish, but is distributed with a soft rubber. The rubber sometimes consists simply of a piece of cloth, or list, or of a small ball of cotton wool or wadding inclosed in a piece of linen rag. The cloth rubbers are formed by coiling a narrow strip of cloth from which the selvedge or list has been torn to a diameter of two or three inches, according to the size of the work in hand. The soft edge, which is left by tearing off the list must be moistened with the polish and applied to the work, or, if preferred, a linen rag may be placed over it, which can be renewed at any time.

French polish is made in many ways, but the simplest and perhaps the best is formed by dissolving two pounds of shellac in one gallon of spirits of wine without heat. The amateur can easily make his own polish, and in any convenient quantities; say two ounces of shellac in half a pint of spirits of wine as a minimum. If by evaporation the polish become too thick, fresh spirit can be added, but if made too thin in the first instance, delay may be occasioned by having to dissolve additional lac before the polish can be used. The proportions already recommended will be found satisfactory.

The surface to be polished must be rubbed perfectly smooth with the finest glass-paper, finishing off with that which is nearly worn out. The dust must be wiped off with a clean cloth, and the surface should be carefully examined, and any scratches removed.

If the rubber is to be made of wadding, the latter must be pulled to pieces, and all the hard knotty portions rejected. A rubber of about an inch and a half in diameter will be large enough for a surface of three or four square feet in extent. The wadding should be thoroughly saturated with polish, squeezed moderately dry, and placed in the centre of a single thickness of soft linen rag, which is then gathered up behind and tied. A few drops of linseed oil are placed on the face of the rubber, which is then fit for use.

The rubber may now be applied to, and moved over, the surface of the work with circular strokes of uniform size, the motion being continuous and the pressure very slight. The position of the strokes should be frequently changed in order to distribute the lacker evenly, otherwise some portions of the surface will be too thickly coated, whilst other parts are neglected. The rubber must be kept in motion until the entire surface has received a uniform coat of lacker, occasionally squeezing the rubber gently between the fingers, to cause the polish to exude from it. When it is wished to remove the rubber, it must not be lifted vertically, but should be swept off at the margin of the work, during one of the circular strokes, and it must never be allowed to remain stationary, as it would adhere to the polish and cause a blemish.

The polish must be allowed to become thoroughly hard, and should then be rubbed over with a worn piece of glass-paper, to remove any irregularities in the lacker or rising of the grain of the wood. Several coats must be applied, and treated in every way like the first.

Directly the lacker becomes hardened on the rag of the rubber a new piece must be substituted, as the hard lacker is liable to scratch the tender coat of polish. This opportunity may be taken to re-saturate the wadding, which must, however, be squeezed as dry as on the first occasion.

When the grain of the wood appears to be well filled with the lacker, and the surface even and tolerably bright, the cloudy marks occasioned by the oil which was put on the rubber may be removed, by taking a clean rubber inclosed in a fresh piece of soft linen rag, a few drops of spirits of wine being placed on the rubber instead of lacker. The work must be rubbed very lightly, beginning with circular strokes, and as the surface becomes dry it may be finished with straight strokes in the direction of the grain, passing the rubber quite off the end of the work. The polishing may be considered complete when the rubber is quite dry.

After the lapse of a few days, the polish will be partially absorbed by the grain of the wood, and it will be necessary to apply another thin coat of lacker. The surface must be lightly rubbed with nearly worn-out glass-paper, in order that the last coat of lacker may be laid under the most favourable circumstances. This last, when quite hard, will require, like the one preceding, to be finished with a clean rubber and spirits of wine.

THE END.

*Arthur Robert Peati(?)
from Mama
1867*

ROUTLEDGE'S EVERY BOY'S ANNUAL.

AN ENTERTAINING

Miscellany of Original Literature.

EDITED BY EDMUND ROUTLEDGE.

With Illustrations.

LONDON:
GEORGE ROUTLEDGE AND SONS,
THE BROADWAY, LUDGATE;
NEW YORK: 416, BROOME STREET.
1867.

COX AND WYMAN,
ORIENTAL, CLASSICAL, AND GENERAL PRINTERS, GREAT QUEEN STREET,
LINCOLN'S-INN FIELDS, LONDON, W.C.

CONTENTS.

PAGE

BARFORD BRIDGE; OR, SCHOOLBOY TRIALS. By the Rev. H. C. Adams, M.A.
 1, 65, 129, 232, 257, 321, 385, 449, 544, 577, 676, 705

CHESS . 19, 106, 147, 204, 275, 378, 433, 468, 523, 636, 663, 755

WORDS WHICH HAVE A HISTORY. By the Rev. Frederic W. Farrar, M.A. 24, 82, 171

THE LATHE, AND HOW TO USE IT; OR, THE PRINCIPLES AND PRACTICE OF PLAIN TURNING. By Temple Thorold.
 31, 96, 161, 224, 735

STODARE'S FLY-NOTES; OR, CONJURING MADE EASY FOR JUVENILE AMATEURS. By Colonel Stodare.
 41, 87, 182, 280, 358, 438

JACK-OF-ALL-TRADES. By Thomas Miller.
 52, 117, 153, 209, 289, 367, 404, 496, 513, 615, 641, 723

CHARADES, REBUSES, ETC. 60, 123, 190

OPEN THE WINDOW, AND CLEAN UP. By R. M. Ballantyne . 111

ANSWERS TO CHARADES, REBUSES, ETC. 128, 160, 254

RECOLLECTIONS OF HARROW. By an Old Harrovian.
 178, 216, 300, 341, 485, 529, 594, 656, 756

REGINALD WARRENDER; OR, EARLY DAYS AT ETON. By William H. G. Kingston 193, 306, 346

THE LATHE.

THE LATHE, AND HOW TO USE IT;

OR,

THE PRINCIPLES AND PRACTICE OF PLAIN TURNING.

BY TEMPLE THOROLD.

CHAPTER I.—THE LATHE.

WHAT could we do without the lathe or its combinations? What could James Watt and his followers have done without its aid? From an engineering point of view, we think we may safely answer, nothing.

If the turner's art were unknown, mechanical science, as a practical, realizable fact, could scarcely exist. The steam-engine would only be a wonderful something that worked beautifully in theory, and would be sure to do so in practice, if the parts that required to be round could but be made truly circular.

So unfortunate a state of things, happily for us, does not exist; if it did, you may be quite sure, printing by machinery would be unknown, and that you could not buy ROUTLEDGE'S MAGAZINE FOR BOYS for fourpence, or even for three times fourpence.

The lathe is of very ancient origin. Pliny ascribes the invention of the turner's craft to Theodore of Samos, and refers to one Thericles who was celebrated as a skilled turner. The ancients were in the habit of saying, it must have been formed in the lathe, when speaking of the workmanship of any object that was wrought with great delicacy and accuracy.

In the Old Testament we find mention of the potter's wheel, which, in principle, is closely allied to the lathe; but the spindle or mandrel of the former is held in a vertical instead of a horizontal position, as in the latter.

The simplest form of lathe that can be employed, for turning objects which are to be wrought only on the outside, is the *pole-lathe*, which consists simply of two horizontal centres, fixed exactly opposite each other, in suitable supports of either metal or wood. One of the supports is permanently secured to a bench or table, but the other is movable, and can be fixed temporarily at the proper distance from its fellow, the distance being determined by the length of the object to be turned. The object or work is suspended between the centres, which penetrate a little way into its extremities, in order to hold it firmly, at the same time allowing it to rotate freely on its axis. Motion is imparted to the work by means of a gut or line, which is coiled round it a few times near one end. The upper extremity of the line is fastened to an elastic pole or lath overhead, and the lower end is secured to a treadle or foot-board, or is simply formed into a loop for the workman's foot. The action is very simple, and may easily be understood. When the operator depresses the treadle, the line which is coiled round the work unwinds in favour of the lower length, but the upper length is shortened by the same amount, thereby causing the work to revolve. This action draws down the elastic pole or lath, which, when the workman raises his foot, returns to its former position, and causes the work to rotate in the opposite direction. A rest or support for the cutting tool is secured to the bench at a convenient distance from the work, and slightly below the centre.

When the work is set in motion by depressing the treadle, it must revolve towards the rest, and on firmly holding a suitable tool thereon, and applying its edge to the revolving work, the prominences of the latter may gradually be removed, until a truly circular form is obtained. As the work rotates in the opposite direction when the foot is raised, the edge of the tool must be slightly withdrawn, otherwise its edge would be injured. This alternate backward and forward motion is inconvenient, and occasions much loss of time; but so great is the simplicity of the machine that it still continues to be favourably regarded by the turners of such simple articles as the legs of chairs, tables, balusters, &c., in soft wood. It is also used in Spitalfields by the bobbin-turners, who work in alder, &c.

The watchmaker's lathe, commonly called a *turn-bench*, or a *turns*, is a small copy of the pole-lathe, but it is very delicate in its construction, and is made entirely of metal. When the work is very small in diameter, as is often the case with the spindles or *arbors*, as they are technically termed by watch and clock makers, the cones, or male centres, cannot be used. Hollow or female centres are substituted for them, and the extremities of the work are pointed instead, and rest in the counter-sinks, or female centres. When the end of the work requires to be turned, it cannot be placed in the hollow centre, but is laid in a shallow groove formed in the circumference of the piece of round steel that forms one of the centres of the *turns*. If the height of the centre cannot be so regulated as to bring the work level, a flat or step must be filed in the centre, which is thus made half round for a little distance from the end. The groove is then made in the flat, and the work lies partly imbedded therein; about half its diameter, however, is above the level of the flat, and can be operated upon by either a file or a cutting tool. A small brass sheave or pulley is fixed on the work, and rotary motion is imparted by means of a light bow, the string of which is coiled once round the pulley. The string is generally a piece of very fine gut, but sometimes a horsehair is used for delicate work. The operator moves the bow in a slanting direction, holding the lower end, which is next him, between the thumb and forefinger of the left hand. The tool, which is held in the right hand, is applied while the work revolves towards him, and is slightly raised during the reverse motion.

Although the general principles of the lathe may be said to exist in the pole-lathe and turns, yet many of the most important operations of turning could not be executed in them. The mandrel, or chuck-lathe, which consists of a horizontal spindle, that revolves with great truth in suitable bearings or supports, possesses not only all the capabilities of the pole-lathe as regards the external turning of work, but also enables us to hollow out or bore the object, if desired. This is effected by securing the work to the end of the mandrel, which, for this purpose, is allowed to project a little way beyond the support. By this arrangement the right-hand centre, which is essential in the pole-lathe and turns, may temporarily be dispensed with, and the face of the work be left clear for the tools.

A suitable pulley is permanently fixed to the mandrel, and occupies the space between the bearings. Rotary motion is imparted to the mandrel in different ways, according to the size of the lathe and the power required to be transmitted. The foot-lathe, which is employed for turning small and light works, is driven by the operator pressing his foot upon a treadle, which is in communication, by means of a short rod, with a cranked axle, carrying a grooved wheel considerably larger than the pulley on the mandrel. The motion transmitted from the treadle to this grooved (fly) wheel is communicated to the pulley by a line or gut; the action is precisely similar to the knifegrinder's wheel, which may frequently be seen in the streets.

When more power is required than can be derived from the treadle, a large hand-wheel, several feet in diameter, is situated at some little distance behind the lathe. A boy is generally hired to turn this wheel, which he does by means of a winch-handle. An endless line, crossed like the figure 8, effects the communication between the driving-wheel and the mandrel pulley. Large and heavy works demand more power than can be obtained from the hand-wheel; consequently, horse, water, or steam power is employed, according to circumstances. The lathe is then called a *power-lathe*.

The wood-turner's lathe is generally made of hard wood, and is of very simple construction. The support for the mandrel is fitted with metal bearings, in which the latter revolves with very little friction. As long works require to be supported at both ends, a movable block, fitted with a centre in the manner of the pole-lathe, is added. The bench, or *bed*, as it is technically called, upon which the supports are fixed, is also made of wood, which answers the purpose sufficiently well; it would, however, be unsuitable for a lathe intended for metal turning.

Having thus briefly noticed the general principles of the lathe, we will now consider the form of this useful tool best adapted to the requirements of an amateur who may be desirous of taking his first lessons in the art of turning.

Fig. 1 represents the front elevation of a mandrel foot-lathe adapted for general light hand turning in both wood and metal. With the exception of the foot-board, T, of the treadle, the lathe should be constructed entirely of metal.

A A, the *bed*, which is a strong cast-iron frame, in construction somewhat like a long narrow box turned bottom upwards. The bottom, or, as it becomes in this case, the top or face of the bed, is planed very true and smooth in a planing-machine. In the centre of the bed, and extending throughout its length, is a gap, the use of which we shall consider presently.

B, is the *headstock*, or support for the mandrel, M, upon which latter is secured the *speed pulley*, or *grooved rigger*, C.

D, is the movable support for the back centre, and is distinguished from the headstock by the name, *sliding poppet head*.

E, the ordinary form of hand-rest; it can be fixed in any required position between the headstock and sliding poppet head, and can be raised or lowered to suit the turner's convenience.

S S, are two cast-iron frames, or standards, in the form of the letter A, to which the bed of the lathe is strongly bolted. R R, is the crank axle upon which the grooved speed or fly-wheel, F, is fixed. The axle is made of wrought iron, and is mounted on steel centres, P P, which answer exceedingly well, if properly proportioned to the weight they have to carry, and there is very little friction attending their use. The centres are fixed in cross bars, forming part of the A frames. When the weight on the crank axle is considerable, the centres are apt to wear unsatisfactorily, and may increase the labour of treading very materially. When a very heavy fly-wheel is employed, or when it is necessary to have two wheels, one at each end of the axle, the extremities of the latter should be placed on friction rollers, which will reduce the friction to a minimum. We may perhaps have occasion to speak of this contrivance hereafter.

H H, the axis of the treadle, which, like the crank axle, is mounted on centres, one at each end.. The foot-board, T, is attached to the axis by three iron bars, springing at right angles from the latter; one near each end of the board, and one in the middle. The treadle and crank are frequently connected by a short rod, having a hook formed at each extremity; the lower end of the rod engages a small loop or eye in the centre bar of the treadle, while the upper end actuates the crank. Considerable friction attends this arrangement, and it is very inferior to the endless chain and friction pulley.

I, is an endless chain formed of numerous flat plates, which are punched out of sheet iron. Each link of the chain consists of several plates ranged side by side. The ends of the plates of every alternate link are placed between the plates of its neighbours in the length way, or, in this case, circumference of the chain. Owing to this, half the links are composed of an even, and half of an uneven number of plates. The ends of the plates of the neighbouring links are connected by a pin, which passes through them all, and is then riveted over the two outside plates, to make all secure. The number of plates required to make a link is regulated by the strain to which the chain will be subjected, and also by the limited space the chain must occupy.

The crank pin should be a little longer than the width of the chain, to allow the latter to work freely over it. The chain is placed in communication with the treadle by means of the friction roller, W, which is a cast-iron wheel or pulley, about four inches in diameter. An eye or loop is formed in the centre bar of the treadle frame for the reception of the roller, and an iron pin passes through the sides of the loop for its axis. The roller has a flanger on each side, to keep the chain in place and prevent it from grinding against the sides of the loop.

The line, g, is generally catgut; the ends of which are attached by a steel hook and eye. The hook and eye are formed with sockets, into which the extremities of the gut are screwed. When selecting them, care must be taken to get the correct size, for, if the sockets be too small, the gut will not screw in properly; and if too large, the screw can have but an imperfect hold. If you have a screw-tap that fits the sockets, or cut a bit of soft wood to the right size, and screw it in, you obtain at once an exact pattern or gauge for the correct size of gut. Before attempting to screw in the gut, the extreme ends must be slightly pared to make them taper, and a little oil should be applied.

We must caution our readers against making the line too tight, or, in other words, too short. If this is done, an unnecessary and injurious strain will be thrown on the mandrel bearing, and the hook and eye are very apt to be torn off, especially if the gut shrink, owing to a sudden change of weather.

Some people prefer gutta percha to catgut for lathe-bands. The ends of a gutta percha band can easily be united by gentle heat; the ends should be cut at an angle, in order to make the surface of the joint as large as possible, and then applied to a piece of flat iron that has been made sufficiently hot just to melt the gutta percha without injuring it by burning.

Both ends should be melted simultaneously, pressed together, and then left to cool. This material is liable to break at the joint, and the band unavoidably becomes shorter every time it is reunited. We strongly recommend our readers to give preference to the gut line, which, although much more expensive, will work better, and outlast many gutta percha bands.

An enlarged side view of the headstock, partly in section, is given in fig. 2, and an end elevation in fig. 3.

B B, is the base, which must be planed quite true, in order that the head may rest firmly on the surface of the bed. A strip, E E, solid with the head, fits between the inner edges of the gap which extends throughout the length of the bed, A A, shown in section in fig. 3. It is necessary that the centre of the mandrel, M' M, S, should be exactly parallel to the centre of the bed in the direction of its length. As it is somewhat difficult to insure absolute truth in this particular, the strip, E, is often made a little narrower than the gap to allow of adjustment, which is sometimes effected by thin wedges inserted at two cross corners.

The headstock is secured in its proper position by the two bolts, I I, which screw into the solid metal forming the bottom. The lower ends of the bolts (also screwed) pass through clearing-holes in a plate or rib, that is cast solid with the bed; a washer-plate is slipped over the end of each bolt, two nuts are then added, and screwed up tightly.

H H, form the supports for the mandrel, M' M, the front end of which revolves in a collar, or bush, while the back end turns upon a cone centre, c. The part, C, of the mandrel is enlarged, and made slightly conical, in order that any slackness occasioned by wear may be obviated by the larger end of the cone working towards the small end of the bush, b'. This bush is straight or parallel on the outside, and is formed with a flange or rim, b', which beds against the face of the headstock, H', and prevents the bush from passing through the hole in which it fits.

Mandrel bushes are sometimes made of steel; but this material is very apt to crack in the hardening process, thus spoiling work upon which much time and care have been bestowed. Case-hardened iron is, therefore, frequently employed in preference to steel, when the bush is large, but it does not wear quite so satisfactorily. As we shall have occasion hereafter to speak concerning the processes of hardening and tempering, we need not enlarge at present.

After boring the bush within, and turning it outside to the proper diameter, to fit tightly in the hole that has been bored in the head, H', it must be hardened. The cone, C, on the mandrel, having been turned to fit the bush, it must also be hardened, and then ground in the bush with emery and oil. When the interior of the bush and the mandrel cone fit fairly, the bush should be driven into its hole in the headstock, where the grinding process must be completed, the back centre, R, c, of which we must now speak, being in its place.

The centre of the hole occupied by the screw centre, R, must be precisely in a line with that of the mandrel bush; otherwise, the lathe cannot work properly, and if the inaccuracy exceed a very trifling amount, the hole must be plugged up and rebored. The screw, R, should just fit the hole, but must pass through it without requiring to be driven by a hammer. The lock-nuts, $n\ n$, when screwed up to their respective facings, which must be truly square to the centre of the hole, effectually fix the centre in the required position.

A small hole, say a quarter of an inch in diameter, must be drilled about an inch up from the end, M', for the double purpose of clearing away the metal in front of the extreme point of the centre, and forming a receptacle for oil, which is introduced at the hole O'; this latter hole is temporarily closed with a screw-plug. The conical point must then be hardened, and likewise the end, M', of the mandrel, in which the hollow or counterpart cone is made.

An oil-hole, O, must also be made through the top of the head, for lubricating the front end of the mandrel.

The screw, S, on the *nose* of the mandrel, should have a strong, coarse-pitched thread, to enable it to withstand the wear of constantly changing the *chucks*, and the strain when turning hard materials. The diameter of this screw must be somewhat less than that of the small end of the cone, C, in order to form a sufficient shoulder or collar, f, for the chucks to bed against when screwed home, otherwise they will be apt to get out of truth.

When it is necessary to remove the mandrel, the back centre, R, must be withdrawn; the mandrel can then be slipped back until the cone, C, is clear of the bush, b. The nose, S, being smaller than the internal diameter of the bush, we are enabled to raise the end, M', and remove the mandrel obliquely.

The necessity for the greatest truth and perfection of workmanship will be admitted when it is understood that the mandrel must revolve easily and smoothly, not harder at some points than at others, and yet be entirely free from slackness. The back centre must be set forward until the cone, C, beds fairly in the bush; the lock-nuts may then be slightly tightened. If it is found that the mandrel has been jammed fast, the inside nut must be unscrewed a trifle, and the back one tightened, to draw the centre back. A smart, but not heavy, blow must be administered with a mallet to the end of the nose of the mandrel, and if it then revolves freely and equably, we must try whether there is any *end shake*. This is easily ascertained by standing behind the back centre, holding the pulley in both hands, and endeavouring to move it backward and forward in the direction of its length. If no motion is perceptible, both the lock-nuts must be equally tightened.

We will now turn our attention to the sliding "poppet-head," shown partly in section in fig. 4; fig. 5 is an end elevation of the same. The "supports," P P, and the strip, E E, are similar to the headstock, figs. 2 and 3, and of like material. The supports carry, and are solid with, a cylindrical body or barrel, B B (shown in section), within which slides a wrought-iron cylinder, H H'. The steel centre, C, is formed with a conical neck or stem, d, which fits the interior of the cylinder at the end H'. The other end, H, is bored smaller, and is screwed to act as a nut to the long screw, S S', by which the cylinder is moved in or out, as required. Excepting the part forming the nut, the interior of the wrought-iron cylinder is bored sufficiently large to clear the screw. The screw is turned round in either direction by the hand-wheel, W, which, for convenience, is fitted with a handle, L, although it is frequently worked by taking hold of its circumference.

(To be continued.)

THE LATHE.

THE LATHE, AND HOW TO USE IT;
OR,
THE PRINCIPLES AND PRACTICE OF PLAIN TURNING.
BY TEMPLE THOROLD.

CHAPTER I. (*continued*).—THE LATHE.

AS it is essential that the screw should only rotate, and not move in the direction of its length, a collar, f, is formed near the back end, and bears against a steel plate, $l\,l$, which is secured with small screws to the head. The thread of the screw, S S, terminates at the collar, but a plain cylindrical stem is continued behind the collar, and to this the handwheel, W, is secured. The front face of the wheel-boss bearing against the outer face of the plate, $l\,l$, and the collar, f, resting on the inner face, effectually prevents any movement of the screw in an end-long direction. From this it is easy to understand that by turning the screw round in either direction, we can cause the cylinder, H H, to move in or out, as may be desired.

As the cylinder, H H, would be apt to turn round with the screw, and thus neutralize the action of the latter, a narrow groove, or *key-way*, is made along one side of the cylinder. A key is fixed inside the barrel, B B, near the front end, and projects just sufficiently to engage the groove or key-way. Although the cylinder is made to fit the interior of the barrel, throughout its length, as closely and accurately as possible, yet it is necessary to provide a set-screw, T, to steady it when projecting some distance from the head. A small saddle-piece, r, made of brass, is let into the upper part of the barrel, and is placed between the point of the screw and the cylinder, to save the latter from being bruised.

The centre is shown separately in fig. 6. The shank, D, is slightly conical or taper, and must exactly fit the hole at the extremity of the cylinder, H H, as any slackness would throw the work out of truth if turned between centres. The shoulder of the straight part at the base of the shank must not rest against the end of the cylinder, H H, and a clearance of at least 1-16th of an inch should be allowed between them to enable the shank to find its proper bearings in the hole. The shank is not subjected to much wear, nevertheless the pressure upon it is sometimes sufficient to cause it to sink a little deeper in the socket. If the taper is very slight the shank will jam itself tight in the socket, and as it would disfigure the straight part, or collar, if we endeavoured to remove the centre by force, the small end of the shank should be sufficiently long to come in contact with the extremity of the screw, when the cylinder, H, is drawn nearly home (as seen in fig. 5); the centre will thus be expelled easily, and without injury. If the centre is required for heavy metal turning, it should be large, as shown by the dotted lines; but for general light work it is more convenient when reduced, as represented in the figure.

The centres themselves upon which the work revolves must not be very acute, or the points will be apt to break off when turning hard material, and if too obtuse the work will be liable to fly out of the centres, as they cannot penetrate sufficiently to afford secure support. An angle of about thirty degrees will be found satisfactory for ordinary work. When the character of the work is variable, that is, sometimes heavy or rough and occasionally light and delicate, it will be advisable to be provided with two or three pairs of centres. The pair for light work may with advantage be more acute, say an angle of about twenty-five degrees.

It must be borne in mind that when turning work between centres it is often necessary to change it end for end; therefore it is important that the pair of centres in use be as nearly alike as possible, otherwise the work will be liable to run untrue when reversed. The centres are made of steel, and that in the sliding head is hardened to prevent too rapid wear. As the centre in the mandrel revolves with the work, it is much less subject to attrition, and need only be slightly hardened.

The ordinary form of hand-rest is seen in fig. 7; R is a cast-iron plate, or saddle, made true on the under side that it may lie fairly on the surface of the lathe-bed, B B. The front end of this saddle is furnished with a boss or socket, G, cast in a piece with it, in which the stem, S, of the rest, E E, fits. By this arrangement the rest can be raised, lowered, or placed at any angle to suit the convenience of the operator. A set screw, P, is provided, to secure the rest in any required position; when slackened, the stem, S, is at liberty, but when tightened, the stem is forcibly pressed against the opposite side of the hole in the socket and held fast. The rest, E E S, is made of wrought iron, and owing to its having some resemblance to the letter T, it is called the T rest; it is mostly employed for wood turning.

A cross section of the saddle, R, is exhibited in fig. 8, which also shows the arrangement for holding down. The holding-down bolt, T, screws into a wrought-iron nut, N, formed with a dovetailed head which fits into, and is capable of sliding in, a similarly shaped groove or recess extending throughout the length of the saddle. The plate, W, also of wrought iron, bears against the under side of the lathe-bed, and serves as a strong washer for the shoulder of the handle, L, to press upon when the bolt is screwed up to fix the saddle. When the bolt, T, is slack, the saddle is at liberty, and can be moved along the bed, drawn out or pushed in at right angles to the latter, or can be set slightly at an angle either to the right or left, as may be required.

CHAPTER I'l.

CHUCKS, ETC.

WE must open this chapter by making an apology. Our readers would perhaps like, now that the lathe has been introduced to their notice, to begin their lessons in turning at once. As this, however, is quite out of the question, we must beg to be excused on the plea that there is no "Royal road to learning" turning, or anything else that requires preliminary grounding and investigation. This being our view of the matter, we shall explain some of the apparatus, tools, &c., required in turning plain objects, before asking our readers to take even their first lesson in the turner's craft.

By referring to fig. 2 it will be seen that the nose of the mandrel is screwed, in order that the various *chucks* required in turning may be secured thereto, removed, and changed at pleasure. Any piece of wood or metal screwed upon the nose of the mandrel for the purpose of holding work or tools is called a "chuck," and very numerous are they, and much ingenuity is displayed in the construction of many of the more complex among them.

The *centre-chuck*, figs. 9 and 10, is the first, and one of the simplest of the group absolutely necessary for even the plainest work. The body, or "chuck," B' B, may be either of cast or wrought iron; if the former, increased thickness or diameter must be allowed to secure strength equal to the latter material, which is decidedly preferable for this and similar small chucks. The socket, B', which screws upon the nose of the mandrel, is made a little larger than the part in which the cone, d, of the centre, C, fits. The centre must fit the chuck accurately and tightly, otherwise it will throw the work out of truth, and occasion much trouble. It is sometimes screwed into the chuck, which is quite as satisfactory and certainly much better than a shaky cone, and it can as easily be replaced by a new one. The driver, D′ D, is made of steel, and is square in section, as may be seen in the perspective view of the chuck, fig. 10. It is capable of sliding in or out, so that the arm, D′, which is the means of imparting the motion of the mandrel to the work, may be brought in contact with the *carrier*, which often varies in size with the work.

A set screw, S, penetrates the side of the chuck to secure the driver in any required position.

Another form of driving-chuck often used is represented in fig. 11. The circular plate, P, is generally from four to six inches in diameter, but this of course is regulated by the size of the lathe, and the height of the centre from the top or face of the bed. The centre may be fixed in the plate itself, or can be formed with a taper stem or shank to fit a conical hole made up the mandrel in a similar manner to the cylinder, H′ H, in the sliding poppet head, fig. 4; if the latter plan is adopted, the nose of the mandrel must be larger in diameter than otherwise would be necessary. The driver, D, is formed with a shank having a square to fit the slot, S, and is thus prevented from turning round when we screw up the nut by which the driver is fixed. The length of the square part of the shank is a little less than the thickness of the plate, P; the remainder of the shank is round, and is screwed for the nut, which, being situated behind the plate, cannot be seen in the figure. Two slots in a line, one on each side of the centre, and two drivers sometimes are employed in order to relieve the centre of the strain which is brought upon it when one driver only is used. A boss, or socket, is formed on the back of the plate into which the nose of the mandrel screws; this cannot, however, be seen in the figure.

It may here be well to observe that the size of a lathe is in general regulated by the height of the centres from the face of the bed, and by the length of the latter. The height of the centres limits the diameter of the work, which cannot exceed twice that distance, unless a special provision be made in the bed. This provision consists simply in a U-shaped cavity, called a *well*, or *break*, which is situated immediately in front of the bead stock, and enables us to employ chucks of much larger diameter than the height of the centres would otherwise permit. It will be understood that if the diameter of the work fixed on the chuck be sufficient to dip into the "well," it cannot project far from the face of the chuck without coming in contact with the right-hand side, or wall of the well, which thus limits the depth or thickness of the object to be turned. The diameter of work turned between the centres is, of course, always limited by the height of the latter; it is, therefore, sometimes necessary temporarily to raise the headstock and sliding poppet head by placing under them suitable metal " packing pieces."

The *strut-chuck*, which serves as centre and driver in one, is employed when turning wood between centres. Fig. 12 is a section taken in the direction of the length; fig. 13, an elevation; and fig. 14 is an end view, showing the centre point and knife edges. This chuck must be made of wrought iron or steel; the knife edges, *e e*, and the centre, C, may be of the latter material, which, in forging, can be welded to a wrought-iron body or socket. The centre, C, as usual, supports only, and determines the position of the work, but the knife edges, *e e*, stick into it, and insure its rotation.

A perspective view of one kind of *facing-chuck* is shown in fig. 15. This chuck is often used for holding pieces of wood that are not circular, and too short conveniently to be supported between the centres. The plate is of metal, quite flat, and provided in the centre with a coarse, threaded screw, S, upon which the work is fixed. This screw must be only slightly taper, otherwise the work will speedily become slack. If the screw hole be detrimental and cannot be plugged up after the work is removed from the chuck, some other method of holding the object must be adopted. In general, this chuck is only used for rough or preparatory work, and for holding a piece of hard wood, which is to be hollowed out to serve as a cup-chuck. Sometimes we may require to face a piece of wood on both sides or ends, and it will be found that if the screw, S, is too taper or conical, it will not hold, if the work be removed and again fixed with the same side next the chuck. If the circumference of the work is to be turned, much greater steadiness will be secured by fixing the poppet head as close as convenient, and using the centre in the ordinary way. Unless we wish to hollow out, or bore the work, the presence of the back centre (as it is often called) will generally not interfere with the free use of the tools as applied for simply facing the end of the work.

Figs. 16 and 17 represent another variety of the facing-chuck. The central screw is omitted, and fine short steel points or spikes are fixed in the face of the plate. This chuck is used when a hole in the centre of the work would be detrimental. Even the small holes made by the spikes would be injurious when the face of the work is required to be quite smooth. Sometimes a piece of wood a little thicker than the ength of the spikes, is pressed home, tapped lightly with a small mallet in the neighbourhood of the spikes, to insure its lying "dead" upon the plate, and then faced flat to receive the work. If the work be much smaller in diameter than the wood fixed on the plate, it will be unnecessary to face more than sufficient to receive the work, which must be glued thereto, and then left until the cement has become quite hard. The work may be supported and keep in close contact with the wood while the glue is drying, by fixing the sliding poppet head in a convenient position, and then, having removed the back centre, bringing the end of the cylinder, H' (fig. 4), against the work by turning the handle wheel. A smart blow will disengage the work from the wood to which it was glued, and the opposite side can, if necessary, be glued to the chuck. If the surfaces to be glued are large, it is advisable to place a piece of thin paper, the full size of the work, between the latter and the chuck, to facilitate their separation.

The *cement-chuck*, which is a plain flat plate, having neither screw nor spikes, is sometimes used for holding thin pieces of bone, ivory, &c. The lathe is set rapidly in motion, and the cement, which is in the form of a stick or lump, is held against the revolving plate. The heat occasioned by friction melts the cement, a little of which adheres to the plate. The ivory, or other small work, must quickly be pressed upon the plate, before the cement again becomes hard. Care must be taken to apply the cement very equally, and not in lumps, or thicker in some places than in others, otherwise it will be difficult to chuck the work truly.

We could give a receipt for making turner's cement, but as the amateur will require very little of this composition, it is better to purchase it at the tool-shop.

The simplest form of hollow, or *cup-chuck*, is seen in section in fig. 18. It is generally made of boxwood, and is sometimes strengthened by a metal ring, $r\ r$, which is driven on tightly, to prevent the chuck splitting when subjected to rough usage. The interior is bored slightly taper, or larger at the mouth than at the bottom, so that the work, when driven in, is sure to be held firmly if it fits the mouth properly. Care must be taken not to allow the work too much taper on the part to be inserted in the chuck, otherwise the latter is almost certain to be split or distorted, besides considerably increasing the difficulty of extracting the work, which is very likely to be injured or broken during its removal. It should be borne in mind that very little taper, and a very moderate degree of tightness, are amply sufficient to hold the work if the tools be properly applied.

Unless the wood is very thoroughly seasoned, it is apt to cast, and the collar, c, of the socket will not always screw up fairly to the shoulder of the mandrel (f, fig. 2), thus throwing the chuck out of truth. The only remedy is to pare away the face of the collar where it bears hardest on the shoulder until it again rest in contact all round. Of course the body of the chuck can no longer run true, and we must rebore it before it can be used. As a change in the weather may distort it the next day, and perhaps make it worse than before, we must find some more certain means of effecting a cure.

Instead of forming the socket of wood or in a piece with the body, it should be made separately of metal, and provided with a circular flange or plate, at least two inches in diameter, by which it must be secured with carpenters' screws to the wood intended for the chuck. This plan possesses great advantages, and the threads or screw in the metal socket will outlast many wooden ones, the threads of which are very liable to "strip," or break off long before the body of the chuck is worn out. If we are furnished with three or four metal sockets, we can fix them to pieces of wood of any size convenient for our work, and can in a few minutes with very little trouble remove a socket from a worn-out block, and secure it to a new one.

Fig. 19 is a sectional view of a *spring-chuck*, which is often used for holding very slight work. It is sometimes made of wood, but metal is much to be preferred, not only on account of the greater neatness which may be secured by its use, but also because the latter material does not warp and twist as wood frequently does, on change of weather. The body of the chuck, B, B, is much thinner than in an ordinary cup-chuck (fig. 18), and is turned taper or conical on the outside, the base or largest end being at the mouth. About six small holes, only three of which, $h\ h\ h$, can be seen, are drilled at equal distances from each other on the circumference; and near the bottom of the "cup" or body of the chuck, narrow slits or saw kerfs, $c\ h$, $c\ h$, $c\ h$, are cut from the mouth to join the holes, as shown in the figure. When the work is pressed into the chuck, the latter slightly expands owing to the elasticity derived from the several longitudinal divisions or kerfs, which practically convert the cup into so many flexible fingers that grasp the object with a greater or less degree of tightness, according to the amount of their distension. A strong movable ring, R R, is fitted to the body, partly to prevent its being distorted by any attempt to force in work too large for its capacity, and also to assist in holding the object by compressing the cup more closely round it, by drawing the ring forward towards the mouth. It will be understood that the ring being incapable of expansion, must powerfully compress the cup as it is drawn toward the large end, which yields and clasps the work that has been inserted.

If our readers wish to make a *cheap* spring-chuck, the back and socket, S S, can be made of *well*-seasoned boxwood, and the body, B B, may be constructed from a piece of thick brass tube, into which the former must be tightly driven. The tube should be further secured by six (or more) small screws, *t t*, inserted at regular distances. The tube must be turned conical on the outside as in fig. 19, and also slightly taper inside, largest at the mouth, before the holes, *h, h, h*, and the kerfs, *c, c, c*, are made.

Cup-chucks made of lead are often used by turners of light kinds of brass work. A piece of wood must first be turned to the proper external shape and size of the intended lead chuck, to serve as a pattern with which the impression can be made in suitable sand, which, on withdrawing the pattern or model, will form a cavity, called a mould, to receive the liquid metal.

As lead would be much too soft for the socket to screw on the mandrel, one made of brass must be placed in the cavity left in the mould by that part of the pattern which represents the socket. The end of this brass socket, which is to be united to the body of the chuck, should be formed with a tolerably large square flange with sloping or dovetail sides, in order that the metal may run round them, and hold the socket fast. If the face of the socket flange is filed bright, and covered with a thin coat of either tin or soft solder, the lead will hold the brass much firmer. A little block tin melted with the lead will make it harder and improve the chuck.

Small chucks of about three or four inches diameter are cast solid. With a view to economy, the newly-cast chucks are first employed for small work, and are bored larger and larger until they become too thin, when they are melted and recast.

There is very little, if any, elasticity in lead, and being soft it is easily put out of truth by extracting the work; it is, therefore, generally necessary to bore it afresh every time it is used. Some people who are too lazy to recast their chucks, or neglect to provide a sufficient number for their work, employ what they facetiously call the "thickening tool." If they cannot find amongst their stock a chuck small enough to admit of reboring, the hammer will be freely applied to the face and circumference of the one nearest to the required size until the lead by yielding has reduced the internal diameter sufficiently to bear reboring. This practice, to say the least of it, is slovenly and very unworkmanlike, and should never be adopted by those who pride themselves upon the neatness and good quality of their tools.

Fig. 20 is a perspective view of another variety of cup-chuck, made of cast iron, and employed for holding short pieces of round brass or iron that we cannot advantageously place between the centres. Three strong steel screws, S, S, S, are screwed through the body of the chuck at equal distances apart. The work is held between the points of the three screws, which can be so adjusted as to bring it exactly into the centre. Large chucks of this description are generally fitted with a second row of screws, a little behind and midway between the foremost set, in order to afford additional support to the work. Six screws, three in each row, are quite sufficient, although eight screws are advocated by some people. The screws are formed with capstan heads, through the sides of which holes are drilled, to admit the tapering point of a simple instrument, fig. 25, called a tommy. The diameter of the holes must not exceed one-third the thickness of the head, and when the latter is small, one hole straight through is as much as it will bear. When the head is large, a second hole is made at right angles to the first.

A useful kind of chuck for holding drills and short pieces of round metal is shown in fig. 21. The shank of the drill must fit the hole in the chuck closely, and a slight flat should be filed on one side to enable the point of the screw, R, to obtain a fair hold. Of course the round metal we may wish to turn must fill the chuck, otherwise it will run out of truth when the screw, R, is tightened. Small drills are often required in the course of our work, and as the shanks are made in proportion to the cutting parts, it will be found very convenient to have two or three small socket chucks formed with shanks, S, fig. 22, to fit into the larger chuck, fig. 21. The large chuck might conveniently have a hole or socket of about five-eighth inch diameter, and the smaller chucks, say three-eighths and a quarter of an inch respectively.

The larger chuck, fig. 21, may be made of cast iron, but the small ones should be either of wrought iron or gun-metal. The screws must be of steel, and about two of the last threads at the ends should be turned off, and the tips hardened to prevent them from spreading out or becoming burred by the pressure to which they are subjected. This precaution should always be adopted for cup-chucks, and all set or pinching screws in whatever situation they may be employed, otherwise it will be difficult, after a little service, to remove the screws, as the ends, by spreading, will have become larger than the holes.

The *arbor-chuck*, fig. 23, is generally made of gun-metal. It is used for holding small annular work, such as rings, &c., thus saving the trouble of turning a new arbor, or mandrel, as it is often called, for each variation of size in the work. The arbor must not be formed with much taper, or the work will slip off when the tool is applied to the left-hand side, or towards the socket, S. The socket may be dispensed with, and a shank, as in fig. 22, can be made to fit the drill-chuck, fig. 21, but the liability of getting out of truth is greater in the latter arrangement.

Fig. 24 is a *spanner* made of wrought iron, used for screwing up and removing the chucks that have no projecting parts by which they can be held. Those chucks for which the spanner is to be employed are provided with a hexagonal or six-sided collar to fit the jaws, J J. The centre-chucks, figs. 9, 10, and 11, can be screwed upon and unscrewed from the mandrel by the carrier, D D, and the screws of the cup-chuck, fig. 20, will answer a similar purpose.

Of the tommy, fig. 25, we have already spoken. It must be made of round steel drawn down or made gradually tapering from the bend to the points, which should not be too sharp. One end, as may be seen, is bent at a slight angle to the longer arm, thus enabling us to use it in corners where the straight arm could not be employed.

(To be continued.)

THE LATHE.

THE LATHE, AND HOW TO USE IT;

OR,

THE PRINCIPLES AND PRACTICE OF PLAIN TURNING.

BY TEMPLE THOROLD.

CHAPTER II. (*continued*).—CHUCKS, ETC.

THE *face-plate*, figs. 26 and 27, is usually employed for holding square, rectangular, or irregularly shaped work which obviously cannot be fixed in a cup-chuck. It is generally as large in diameter as the height of the centres will permit, to afford ample space on its surface for the work, and the means of securing the latter. Cast iron is the material commonly employed for face-plates, and, indeed, for most of the ordinary chucks, if they exceed five or six inches diameter, as brass would be too costly, and at the same time less suitable, for a lathe intended for ordinary plain work.

The face, or front side of the plate against which the work is placed, must be very carefully turned, and made quite flat; and its truth in this particular should be tested by a correct steel straight edge, applied across the centre. The edge or rim also must be turned, but the back may remain in the rough, and can be painted, as the hard skin or scale formed in casting increases in some degree the stiffness of the plate. It will be seen, by reference to fig. 26, that the plate is perforated with several slots, or rectangular holes, through which are passed the screw bolts for securing the work. The thickness must be increased, to compensate for the absence of the metal in so many places, otherwise the plate will be distorted, or drawn out of truth, by the unequal strain to which it unavoidably is often subjected by the bolts employed to bind the work to its face. As the bolts can seldom act immediately upon the work by passing through it, rectangular wrought iron plates are used in the manner of clamps. A slot large enough to allow the bolts to pass through easily, occupies the centre of each plate, and extends to within a short distance of the ends. One end of each plate rests upon the work, and the other extremity is supported by a bit of hard wood, or a piece of metal, in order that it may be level. The number of plates to be used depends upon the magnitude and character of the work; two or three are in general sufficient, and we can seldom apply more than four advantageously. The bolts should be formed with square necks immediately under the heads, to fit the slots in the face-plate, to prevent them from turning round when the nuts are being screwed up. This simple device saves much trouble, and the left hand is at liberty to support the work, if necessary, until the bolts take hold, instead of being engaged with a second spanner to keep the bolt heads steady while the nuts are being tightened.

It not unfrequently happens that we require to face the work throughout, and as the ends of the plates would prevent this, another method of holding it must be adopted. Four contrivances called *dogs*, each armed with a steel set-screw, which takes effect on the margin of the work, are secured to the face-plate.

The dog is very simple in construction, consisting substantially of a rectangular piece of wrought iron somewhat wider and thicker than the width of the slots in the face-plate, as it must not pass through them. It is provided at one end with a screw shank with a square neck about the same size as the ordinary bolts used with the plates. The length or height of the dog above the surface of the face-plate need not be greater than the head of the set-screw renders necessary. This screw is "tapped" or screwed through the widest side of the dog, and must be parallel to the surface of the face-plate, or, what is the same, at right angles to the shank by which the dog is secured in its place.

The dogs are fixed opposite one another, one in each of the four longest slots of the face-plate. They can be placed at any distance from the centre, within the length of the slots, that the shape of the work may render desirable. The closer the dogs can be fixed to the margin of the work the better, as the set-screws act with greater effect when their points do not project far from the dogs.

It may be observed that separate dogs, plates, &c., are usually only employed for securing metal works to the face-plate, as wood can be glued to a temporary wood facing attached to the face-plate with ordinary carpenter's screws, or in the manner already described under fig. 16.

The *dog-chuck* proper, figs. 28 and 29, is one of the most useful of the chucks employed by the plain metal turner. Fig. 28 is a perspective view, showing the front of the chuck and the four dogs, D, D, D, D. The plate itself is made of cast iron, and is about the same size as the face-plate, and, like it, must be very carefully turned. Only four slots, one for each dog, are made through the chuck. The dogs, as may be seen in the engraving, are much wider than the slots, and they are formed with square blocks, which accurately fit their respective slots; the latter being made quite true and parallel inside to afford as much steadiness as possible to the dogs. A screw stem or short bolt is formed solid with the square block on each dog, and when the latter is put in its place a small iron plate about a quarter of an inch thick, having a hole in the centre a trifle larger than the screw stem, is slipped over the latter; a nut is then placed on the stem and screwed down to the plate, thus fixing the dog.

As all this takes place behind the chuck, it will be better understood by referring to the back view, fig. 29. The nuts for fixing the dogs are seen at n, n, n, n, and the plates against which they are screwed at P, P, P, P. A raised strip or facing is made on each side of the slots for the plates to bear upon. One of each pair is represented at F, F, F, F; they must be very carefully wrought, and must be quite parallel to the front of the chuck, otherwise the dogs will be slack in some positions and stick fast in others. The dogs are moved up and down within the range of the slots by four strong screws, C, C, C, C, one to each dog. These screws are so fitted as to be incapable of moving in the direction of their length, and can only be turned round, either to the right or left as may be required, to move the dogs towards or from the centre of the chuck. The ends of the screws, K, K, K, K, fig. 28, are formed with squares, and the socket, K, of a suitable key or spanner, fig. 30, is slipped over them, by which means we obtain the necessary leverage, and can alter the position of any of the dogs separately at pleasure.

The outer circumference of the dogs, R, R, R, R, is intended for carrying annular or hollow cylindrical work, which is slipped over them; they are then drawn from the centre by means of their respective screws until they bear with the requisite pressure against the inner circumference of the work. The inner circumferences of the dogs give two sizes, the larger at I, I, I, I, and the smaller at B, B, B, B; these are for holding work externally. It will be seen that the outer and inner circumferences of the dogs are roughened or chequered to enable them to grip the work firmly.

Even when the dogs are brought as close to the centre of the chuck as their corners will permit, they cannot hold work that is smaller in diameter than about the size of the mandrel nose. This may be obviated by attaching to them with screws four temporary pieces or auxiliary dogs, for which purpose two screwed holes, s, s, are made in each of the dogs proper, as may be seen in fig. 28. These pieces are about thick enough to fill the recess or step in the dogs, and make them level throughout. One end of each piece bears against the step, I, of the dogs, and the screws are thereby relieved of a great part of the strain that otherwise would be brought upon them when the dogs are in use. The holding-ends may be bored sufficiently small to hold work about half-an-inch in diameter, if desired, but the cup-chuck, fig. 20, is generally preferred for this purpose. The auxiliary dogs are generally employed when the smaller circumference of the dogs proper is required to hold work that must not touch the face of the chuck, a space, perhaps, of half-an-inch being left between them to allow the tool to pass quite through the work without danger of injuring the chuck by cutting a groove or furrow in it. In this case the holding ends of the separate dogs are generally bored to the same size as those of the dogs proper. The dogs are usually made of wrought iron case-hardened, which is tougher than hardened steel, and quite as serviceable in this position. Neither iron nor steel would long retain its shape at the holding points, if unhardened, and the checkering would soon be rendered useless.

When long and slender work is turned between the centres, an additional support must be provided to impart the requisite steadiness. This support or bearing, shown in fig. 31, consists of a cast-iron frame, F, F, furnished with a block of hard work, W, W, through which is bored a hole, B, the exact diameter of the work. The wood, seen separately in fig. 32, is held in position by the V or wedge-shaped formation of the inner sides of the frame F, which fit into corresponding grooves in the wood. After fitting the solid block of wood into the frame, the cap or plate, C, C, is placed above it, and the nuts are then screwed down.

The height of the frame must be such that the centre of the wood shall coincide with the centres of the lathe. The exact position of the centre for the hole may easily be found by fixing the frame temporarily in its place, and then securing the poppet head close to it, and screwing out the centre against the wood, which will be marked by the point. A pair of dividers or compasses must be set to the radius, or half the diameter of the required hole, and with them a circle must be distinctly marked.

If the face of the wood on the side opposite to that on which we have made the circle be true, and at right angles to the lathe bed, the wood can be fixed on the face-plate, and the hole be very easily bored. The wood is adjusted on the plate by the circle, which must run exactly true before attempting to make the hole. Before replacing the wood in the frame, it must be cut in half across the centre of the hole, and parallel to the bed of the lathe. The two halves can then be brought closer together as the hole becomes too large by wear.

This bearing frame can be fixed in any required position between the heads, and must be placed as close as possible to that part of the work which is being turned, in order to prevent it springing from the edge of the tool. The end of the work next the poppet head must be turned for a short distance to fit the hole in the bearing before the latter can be employed, and after fixing it, the work must be reduced to the same diameter throughout its length, and the bearing must occasionally be moved towards the vicinity of the tool. The holding-down bolt, which is similar to that of the poppet-head, passes through the hole, H, in the base of the frame, fig. 31, and is furnished with a washer-plate and nut.

The *carrier*, fig. 33, is a simple contrivance made of wrought iron, which is employed in conjunction with the driver, D, figs. 9 and 11, for imparting the rotative motion of the mandrel to metal-work, when the latter is fixed between centres. The end of the work is placed within the bow or loop of the carrier, and the set-screw is then screwed down upon it. If the end of the work would be injured if bruised by the point of the set-screw, it must be protected by wrapping a piece of thin sheet copper or tin round it before inserting it in the carrier. The stem or shank of the carrier must rest against the driver, which, as we have already shown, is capable of being fixed closer to or further from the centre, to enable it to engage carriers of various sizes.

Fig. 34 represents the *drilling-plate*, which is very useful when we wish to employ the lathe as a drilling machine. The stem, D, fits into the end of the cylinder, H', of the poppet-head, fig. 4, and the work to be drilled is held against the plate, P, which must be quite flat. The drill, according to its size, is held in the drill-chuck, fig. 21 or 22. The poppet-head is fixed close to the drill, just allowing sufficient space between its point and the face of the plate, P, to introduce the work. The lathe is set in motion, and the hand-wheel, W W, figs. 4 and 5, is turned round very slowly, great care being required to avoid too much pressure upon the drill. Great force can be exerted by means of the hand-wheel screw, and many drills will be broken at first; but a little practice will conquer all difficulties. We shall notice drilling fully hereafter.

Sometimes, after fixing metal work in the chuck, it may be necessary to find the centre of the object before proceeding to use any of the tools, and even after the work has been partly wrought we may require to make or cut a deep centre to receive the point of a drill, &c. The centre can either be marked or cut with a graver, or diamond-pointed tool, but some practice is needed before even this apparently easy operation can successfully be accomplished. Little or no skill is demanded in the employment of the *broach-centre*, fig. 35, which can be used with the greatest ease and certainty. This centre is made like an ordinary cone-centre, and must be of the same angle: the stem, D, also must fit the end of the cylinder, H, fig. 4. Before hardening the cone, A B B, it must be marked out into four equal parts, and four flats filed, leaving the lines of division standing as four sharp edges; it must then be hardened and tempered like an ordinary cutting tool for metal.

When about to use this centre, it must be placed in the cylinder of the poppet-head, which latter should be fixed as close as convenient to the work on the chuck. The lathe is then set in motion, and the point of the centre is very gently pressed against the work by turning the hand-wheel slowly round until a centre of the required depth is made.

The *boring-collar*, or *cone-plate*, exhibited in figs. 36 and 37, is an important addition to the apparatus required in turnery operations. It consists of a cast-iron plate, P P, turned quite flat on both sides, and circular on the edge or circumference. Several conical holes, varying in size, are carefully bored through the plate, all the centres being equidistant from the centre of the pin, or axis, B, upon which the plate is capable of rotating. This pin, which is made either of iron or steel, fits a hole in the boss of the cast-iron support, or bracket, H H, shown partly in section in fig. 36. It will be observed that the pin is formed with a head at B, which prevents the plate slipping off, and draws it closely to the face of the bracket on screwing up the nut, N. A transverse section of the plate also is exhibited, in fig. 36, taken through the centre of the conical holes, C and D. The centres of the holes which are represented by the dotted circle in fig. 37 must correspond exactly with the lathe centres when, by turning the plate round, they are respectively brought into the highest position. The base or foot of the bracket, H H, is formed like that of the poppet-head, and a piece, E E, fits in the opening along the centre of the bed, to assist in keeping it steady, and to insure its central position.

The boring-collar is used to support the end of cylindrical work when we require to bore it, as the back-centre cannot then be employed. If the object is fixed either in the cup-chuck or the dog-chuck, and does not project much, it will probably be sufficiently steady to bear boring without the assistance of the boring-collar. In the case of long work, however, or such as is supported only by the mandrel centre, either the boring-collar, or a bearing similar to fig. 31, is absolutely necessary.

The end of the work must be faced, and the circumference, or exterior, turned for a short distance from the extremity previously to placing it in the boring-collar, otherwise it will not only run untrue, but also injure the conical hole in which it revolves.

Everything being in readiness, the bracket, H H, figs. 36 and 37, is placed on the bed of the lathe, the large ends of the conical holes being towards the mandrel. The nut, N, is then slackened to allow the plate, P, to turn, if it be requisite to bring any particular hole opposite the end of the work. In selecting the hole, it is necessary to ascertain, by trial, before securing the bracket, whether the work can pass through the small end, and if it does, a smaller cone must be tried. If the work enters the hole about an eighth of an inch at the large end, or is within the same distance of the most contracted part, it will be favourably situated, and indeed any position between these may be adopted.

As the centre of the hole must correspond exactly with the lathe centres in all directions, not only as regards height, which is determined by the pin, B, and the bracket, H H, but also sideways—to ensure the latter, a mark, or line, must be made from the centre of each hole on the side of the plate next the bracket, and one line must be drawn across the top of the boss of the bracket in the direction of its length. Supposing all these lines to be correctly placed, the centre of any one of the conical holes will tally with the centres of the lathe as the lines on the plate are brought in turn precisely opposite the line on the bracket: the nut, N, must then be screwed up tightly to fix the plate.

The bracket not having yet been secured, we can slide it along the bed towards the mandrel until the end of the work takes its proper bearing in the conical hole which has been chosen for its reception. The work must be free to revolve easily, but without "end-shake." After screwing down the nut of the bolt that holds the bracket, we can shift the latter a trifle in either direction by striking it smartly on the foot with a hammer, if the work has been set fast, or has gained too much freedom by any movement of the bracket while securing it. The end of the work revolving in the conical hole must be kept well lubricated with oil, otherwise the friction will cause the bearing surfaces to "cut," or wear into deep furrows, which will speedily ruin them.

Before bringing this chapter to a close we will notice a method of fixing rectangular work on the face-plate, when it is necessary to face it on two or more sides which must be square, or at right angles to one another. A perspective view of this arrangement is given in fig. 38. To the face-plate, F, is bolted a cast-iron angle-plate, P D; the nuts by which it is secured are seen at *b b*. This angle-plate, or *angle-chuck*, is planed on the two outer faces, which must be exactly at right angles to each other, or the work executed upon it will not be square. The edge of that side of the chuck which is placed next the face-plate is rounded to the same radius as the plate itself, as the corners would be in the way, and might not clear the lathe-bed.

The work—a square block of iron or brass—is represented at W. It is secured to the angle-chuck by two wrought-iron plates, *l l*, and two bolts, which pass through the latter, and through suitable slots in the chuck. The slots in the angle-chuck are the same width as those in the face-plate, therefore the same bolts can be employed with both.

The upper surface of the angle-chuck upon which the work, W, is fixed, must be sufficiently far from the centre of the face-plate to allow of the work being placed centrally. Of course that part of the work on which we intend to operate must project beyond the edge of the angle-chuck a little more than the aggregate thickness of the several cuts we must take to reduce the work to the required dimensions. The outer ends of the plates, *l l*, are supported by bits of hard wood, or metal of the same depth or thickness as the work; one of these pieces is seen at T, fig. 38.

Before the work can be properly secured to the angle-chuck, its under face which is to rest thereon must be filed, or otherwise made perfectly flat, in order that it may have a firm bearing and also serve as a true "foundation," from which the four sides required to be at right angles to it can be wrought.

The first side having been faced, the bolts that hold the work must be slackened, and the latter turned round, the finished surface being placed against the face-plate. If the work be not thick enough to overhang the front edge of the angle-chuck sufficiently for turning, a parallel bit of metal can be put between it and the face-plate to make up the deficiency, but the piece thus introduced must be perfectly parallel, otherwise it will throw the work out of truth.

The side parallel to that now resting on the angle-chuck, and on which the plates, *l l*, bear, may next be wrought, the side last faced being set upon the angle-chuck, and the original "foundation" placed towards the face-plate.

Four out of six sides are now supposed to have been completed, the first or original "foundation," which we filed true, and the three faced in the lathe. One of the two remaining sides must be set in the proper position for facing with a square, the back of which is applied to the face-plate, and the outer edge of the blade to the finished sides. If the bolts for fixing the work hinder us from using the square in this way, they must temporarily be removed, and a line scratched across the surface of the angle-chuck, and at right angles to the face-plate, by drawing a scriber or sharp-pointed steel wire along the edge of the blade of the square. This line must be so placed as to allow the centre of the work to coincide with that of the face-plate when the edge of the work is adjusted to the line. When this side is finished, the last may be set by the line, or in the manner previously described.

A circular lump of lead having a bolt-hole through it should be secured to the face-plate opposite the angle-chuck to counterbalance the weight of the latter, which, being out of the centre, would otherwise cause the lathe to run very irregularly. If the lead is fixed close to the edge or circumference of the face-plate, it will act with greater effect in counterbalancing the chuck than when situated near the centre; its influence therefore can in this way be slightly regulated.

The angle-chuck is shown separately in figs. 39, 40, and 41. Fig. 39 represents the surface on which the work is fixed, and the dotted line shows the thickness of the right-angled side that is bolted against the face-plate; in fig. 40 is seen the outer edge of the plate, fig. 39, and the inner side of that which is at right-angles to it; fig. 41 is an end view of the chuck.

Angle-plates, which are exactly similar to the angle-chuck, are frequent additions to the turner's apparatus, and some people employ them for carrying wood bearings, instead of using the frame, F F, fig. 31. The wood is required much larger than when fixed in a frame, as it must be secured with bolts to the front of the angle-plate. A suitable piece of wrought-iron plate, with a conical hole near one end, and a bolt-hole or slot at the other, for fixing it to the angle-plate, serves as a boring-collar. As one conical hole only can be bored in this plate, a new plate must be provided if any variation in the work renders the former unsuitable. Angle-plates which are to be employed on the lathe-bed should be provided with a strip, similar to E E, on the poppet-head, figs. 4 and 5, to prevent it shifting sideways, and insure its central position.

(To be continued.)

THE LATHE.

Some of these designs are copied from Messrs. Holtzapfel's large work, "Turning and Mechanical Manipulation," which excellent book we can cordially recommend to our readers.

THE LATHE.

Some of these designs are copied from Messrs. Holtzapfel's large work, "Turning and Mechanical Manipulation," which excellent book we can cordially recommend to our readers.

THE LATHE, AND HOW TO USE IT;
OR,
THE PRINCIPLES AND PRACTICE OF PLAIN TURNING.
BY TEMPLE THOROLD.

CHAPTER III.—HAND-TURNING TOOLS.

SOME of our friends may remember that we warned them, in the early pages of "Our Workshop," against purchasing "boxes of tools." Advice, though good, unfortunately is seldom well received, because people generally are in too great a hurry to become possessed of something that may have taken their fancy, and accordingly resent any well-meant hint that was not solicited, especially if a caution be implied.

Even though gratuitous advice might be unpalatable to some folk, we should not hesitate, but bestow our counsels most impartially, and take the risk of offending a few. Happily, in this instance, however, there is no danger of anything we may say being taken amiss, simply because our readers will not get the advice for nothing, but must pay for it: this will insure its favourable reception.

A good lathe necessarily is an expensive machine, and we most strenuously counsel our amateur friends to take time, and watch their opportunities, and not buy the first lathe that may appear desirable, because "cheap." Except under peculiar circumstances, a "cheap lathe," like other cheap wares, is the costliest rubbish that can be placed as lumber in a workshop.

It should be borne in mind that although wood may more generally be employed than metal during the earlier efforts of the young turner, yet, as he gains experience, works in metal will open a far wider field for practice and the exercise of skill.

The wood-turner's lathe, which usually is made almost entirely of wood, is far too primitive to be useful to the amateur, who necessarily requires his lathe to be as universal as possible. This, at first sight, would appear to demand a large original outlay, but if the amateur exercises a little judgment, this to a great extent may be avoided. When choosing his turning-machinery he should adopt what may be called the "accumulative method," which admits of future additions being made to most of the apparatus and tools needed in the higher branches of the art.

For general plain turning in wood and metal, such as an amateur mechanical engineer is likely to practise, a neat, substantial lathe, made entirely of metal, is earnestly recommended, as being the best. The top or surface of the bed should be quite flat, as the *compound slide-rest*, and other useful apparatus which hereafter may be procured, can be fitted to it with great facility and accuracy. The utility of the lathe, and the value of the slide-rest, will be greatly enhanced if the mandrel head-stock is furnished with an arrangement of toothed wheels called the *back-gear*, by means of which greater power and much slower motion is secured when turning metal works of large diameter, and without inconveniently reducing the speed of the fly-wheel. If, at the time of purchasing a lathe, you neglect to obtain one fitted with a geared head-stock, the expense of afterwards substituting the latter for the simple pulley will be much greater than the extra cost of a lathe originally so fitted.

The size of the lathe is a matter that also requires consideration. If the centres are five inches above the surface of the bed, they will be sufficiently high to admit a piece of wood or metal as large as can conveniently be turned in a lathe driven by the foot. The bed should be from three feet six inches to four feet in length, and must be supported by two strong cast-iron standards, to which it is securely bolted.

The next and most difficult question, that of price, comes between the would-be turner and his ardent desire—a good lathe. We do not require to be told that very few of our readers can afford ten or fifteen pounds; and this is a very moderate sum to give for a fair average lathe, unfurnished with a slide-rest, if purchased new of a good maker. As it is idle for an amateur to entertain for a moment the idea of making a lathe for himself, he must patiently wait until he can find a second-hand article within his means.

Excellent lathes and other tools may often be bought for half of their value, at sales by auction; but the greatest caution must be exercised in order to avoid the unpleasant consequence of a very bad, instead of a good, bargain. Do not trust to your own unaided judgment, but take the advice of some friend who has had experience in such matters; and if you are unacquainted with any one qualified to help you, it will be economy on your part to give a practised metal-turner or engineer a trifle for a practical opinion on the merits of your proposed purchase.

Favourable opportunities for buying really good second-hand machinery are by no means rare. Not long since, a friend of ours wanted a good lathe, and, as usual, cheap. We recommended him to watch for advertisements of sales by auction of engineers' tools, and promised to give all the assistance in our power. His patience, in this instance, was not very sorely tried, and he obtained, for little more than half-price, a new screw-cutting and universal self-acting lathe, that had been made expressly to meet the requirements of amateur mechanical engineers. We are aware that this was an unusually fortunate circumstance, but know that on several other occasions very satisfactory purchases have been made, and can speak, therefore, from experience.

The gouge, shown in two views, figs. 42 and 43, is employed by the wood turner to remove the irregular or rough exterior of the work, and to reduce it to the circular form previously to applying the chisel. The body of the gouge somewhat resembles a reed or quill split in half in the direction of its length, or may be compared to a hollow chisel: a transverse section is seen at S. The cutting-edge is ground exteriorly and obliquely to an elliptical figure, and differs in shape from the carpenter's gouge.

The turning chisel, figs. 44 and 45, unlike the carpenter's chisel, is ground with a double bevel, or from both sides, and the cutting edge is not at right angles to the shaft, but obliquely, as in fig. 44.

The turner's gouges and chisels vary in width from one-eighth inch to two inches, and as they are not used with force, or driven with a hammer, no shoulders are formed on the tangs, as the latter are not likely to sink too deeply into or split the handle. When the gouges and chisels exceed one inch in width, they generally are fixed in long handles, as in the figures, which measure, including the tools, from fifteen to twenty-four inches; the smaller tools have shorter handles, from eight to twelve inches in length over all.

The same tools cannot advantageously be employed upon both hard and soft woods, and the tools suitable in each case are somewhat differently applied. The bevels of the cutting edges of tools used for turning soft wood are ground at an angle varying from twenty to thirty degrees, and those for hard wood are more obtuse, being usually about forty degrees. The angle at which the cutting edge is formed should be regulated by the nature of the substances to be wrought, and it may be accepted as a rule, that the harder the material the more obtuse, and the softer the more acute must be the angle of the bevel. This principle is borne out both in carpentry and turnery, but is carried to a much greater extent in the latter when metal work is executed.

The position of the gouge for turning soft wood is represented in fig. 46. The centre of the back or convex part of the gouge, G, lies upon the rest, R, which is sufficiently raised to allow the bevel indicated by the dotted line, a, b, to lie upon the circumference of the cylinder, W, or be nearly as a tangent to it. The handle of the tool is grasped near the end in the right hand, the thumb being extended as seen in fig. 47; and if the cut is to be light, the left hand is placed under the convex part of the gouge, and the fingers are closed round it, their tips resting on the right hand side-edge, while the thumb presses upon the other to keep the instrument closely down to the rest. When the cut is unusually heavy, or the work much out of truth, the hand generally is placed over, instead of under the shaft, and the fingers are closed beneath it, thus enabling the operator to hold the tool more securely, and, by pressing heavily upon it, prevent it slipping back when a knot or any irregular portion of the work comes suddenly in contact with its edge.

Sometimes in "roughing out," when it is unnecessary to traverse the gouge far along the rest, or in the direction of the axis of the work, the fingers of the left hand are clasped round the neck of the rest, just clear of the work, and the thumb is placed across the top of the gouge, which is thus clamped powerfully down upon the rest. The edge of the tool is made to take effect in the lengthway of the work, by moving the handle alternately to the right and left, the shaft swivelling as it were on a centre under the left thumb, which is kept stationary. In this method the cutting edge of the tool moves in a small arc of a circle, but no inconvenience arises from this circumstance during the first stage of the work, and, if desired, a short rectilinear movement can be imparted to the instrument by alternately bending and extending the thumb.

Under ordinary circumstances, and after the wood has been turned roughly circular, the gouge must be traversed steadily along the rest in order to make the surface of the work as regular as possible, before applying the chisel. Sometimes when using a tool fitted with a long handle, the end of the latter is tucked under the right arm, by which it is firmly pressed to the side, and the hand grasps the handle near the middle. When the end of the handle is held in the right hand only, the latter must be kept close to the workman's side, the tool being moved along the rest by the left hand.

The application of the gouge for facing flat surfaces differs somewhat from that already described for ordinary cylindrical turning. The side-edge of the tool is placed upon the rest, the convex or rounded side, which ordinarily lies thereon, being towards the surface about to be wrought. The handle of the gouge is held nearly horizontal, and at first the bevel of the cutting edge is allowed to touch the work, but before the tool can take effect, the handle must be inclined sideways until, by slightly raising the bevel from the work, the cutting edge is enabled to operate as the instrument is gradually urged from the circumference to the centre of the work.

When the gouge is employed to face the bottoms or interior planes of hollow works, such as shallow cup-chucks, boxes, &c., it is applied in much the same manner as just described for external flat surfaces. The shaft or blade of the tool, however, is more inclined horizontally than in the first operation, and the cut is begun at the centre instead of at the circumference or margin of the work. The middle of the elliptical edge or nose of the gouge is pressed forward until a shallow hole, equal in depth to the intended cut, has been bored; the instrument is then swept across the work by lowering the handle, and at the same time twisting it round one-fourth of a revolution. If the manipulation is properly performed, both the side edges of the gouge will lie upon the rest, when the entire surface or plane has been traversed by the cutting edge, and the tool assumes the position shown in fig. 47, only the rounded or convex part of the shaft will be uppermost.

In fig. 48 it will be seen that the position of the chisel for turning the cylinder, W, when of soft wood, is the same as that of the gouge when similarly employed. The shaft of the chisel, however, is not held strictly at right angles to the axis of the work, but slightly inclined in the opposite direction to that in which it is being moved along the rest. In fig. 49, which is a longitudinal view of the work, the chisel, R, is supposed to be passing from left to right, and L from right to left. The oblique position of the cutting edge prevents its taking too wide a bearing on the work, and also enables it to act with great smoothness, entirely avoiding any risk of "tearing up" the fibre of the wood, which would be very likely to happen if the edge were applied parallel to the axis of the work. The edge may be ground square across, but the blade must then be held in a more slanting position sideways, to keep the corners of the tool from digging into the work.

Those who are acquainted with the construction and use of the joiner's planes will observe in the turner's chisel the same principles as exist in the *skew-rebate* and *fillister*. In these planes the irons are set obliquely in the stocks, and their edges take effect on the flat surface in much the same manner as the slanting edge of the turning chisel, when applied to cylindrical work in the lathe.

The manner of holding the chisel when turning cylindrical work in soft wood is exhibited in fig. 50. The handle is held in the right hand, which must be kept close to the person, as in using the gouge, and the palm of the left hand should be placed on the blade, and the fingers closed underneath it. The chisel is traversed along the rest by moving both hands simultaneously, and sometimes also by inclining the body a little in the required direction. Considerable practice is necessary in the manipulation of the chisel, and at first it will be found difficult to remove the wood in their uniform shavings, and to make the work truly circular.

Fig. 51 represents the manner of holding and applying the chisel for turning or facing the end of the work. The longer side edge of the tool is placed on the rest, and the chamfer or bevel of the cutting edge is brought into agreement with the intended plane by holding the chisel in a slanting position sideways. The handle—which, as usual, is grasped in the right hand—is lowered until the point of the chisel is raised nearly to the level of the centre. The blade of the chisel, as may be seen in fig. 51, lies in the hollow of the left hand, the fingers of which are closed round it, the thumb bearing on the upper side-edge. The rest is so placed as to enable the turner to hook the middle joint of his forefinger under it near the end, and thereby obtain greater control over the tool, which, being supported only on a narrow edge, is apt to swerve from its proper course, and damage the work. As the point of the tool is thrust from the margin to the centre of the work, a very thin slice of wood is detached, which curls over towards the back-centre, as it is displaced by the outer chamfer of the chisel. The chisel must be held very firmly, and kept rigidly to its work, especially at the commencement of the cut, as it is very apt to be drawn over the circumference of the wood, in which it will make a deep spiral or screw-like groove that may unfit it for the purpose for which it was intended. This is the most difficult manipulation of the chisel, and even after considerable practice a little want of caution may cause the chisel to slip and rip off the edge or corner of the work, and entirely destroy its artistic finish.

When boring work, the rest is placed across its face a little below the centre, as shown in fig. 52. The tool is held horizontally, and the thumb of the left hand is placed on its upper edge, to keep the instrument steady on the rest, while it is thrust forward by the right hand. The cutting-edge of the tool should be on a level with the centre; its action, however, is not impeded, if only slightly raised above the centre, but, if lowered, its operation is sooner obstructed.

If the wood is very hard, the tool is apt to fly from the work towards the centre, but it can generally be restrained by hooking the fingers of the left hand under the rest, and pressing more forcibly on the instrument with the thumb.

The position of the tool when boring is the same whether the wood be hard or soft, and its action is that of a scraping rather than a cutting instrument. Hard-wood tools are applied nearly horizontally as shown in fig. 53, and are formed with a single bevel like a firmer chisel, but the angle is much more obtuse, varying from about 40 to 60 degrees. They remove the material by scraping it off in short thin shavings, and are much more suitable for hard-wood turning than the double-bevelled chisels, which are, however, sometimes used upon the hardest woods, and are applied as in fig. 50. An ordinary soft-wood chisel is too keen for turning the harder kinds of woods, and its edge very soon becomes notched; therefore two sets of tools should be provided, and ground to the angles already recommended for each variety of work. Too much attention cannot be given to this branch of the subject, and our readers will soon discover that the angles at which the cutting edges of their tools are ground, influence most materially the production and finish of the work.

We shall have occasion, when speaking of *fixed* or *slide-rest* tools, to notice the angles which in practice have given the best results, and therefore will not enlarge at present.

(*To be continued.*)

THE LATHE, AND HOW TO USE IT;

OR,

THE PRINCIPLES AND PRACTICE OF PLAIN TURNING.

(*Continued from page* 231.)

CHAPTER III. (*continued*).—HAND-TURNING TOOLS.

IN addition to the tools for turning soft wood figured at page 225, we have the hook-tool (fig. 54), which is used for hollowing out the insides of boxes. Like the others, it is chamfered on both sides. Fig. 55 represents the parting tool for rapidly cutting through the work at right angles to its axis. The teeth of course give it a saw-like action. There is also another tool of the shape indicated in fig. 56. It is of great use in trimming up the ends of the work. There are many others of almost an infinite variety of shapes and sizes sold by the various tool-makers, each manufacturer having his set of patterns, but the young amateur should be warned once for all against the needless multiplication of tools. Those enumerated are quite enough for all ordinary purposes, indeed many good workmen content themselves with the gouge and chisel only.

For hardwood, ivory, bone, and other materials of a similar description, a more extensive set of tools will be required. As we have already mentioned, they differ from soft wood tools in having only a single bevel, the beveled side being always kept *downwards* when working. The angle of the bevel is also greater, being from 40° to 60° or 70°, instead of from 20° to 30°. The angle, too, at which the tool is held is also much increased, as may be seen in fig. 53. In fact, the action of the tool is no longer that of a cutting instrument, the material being scraped away in more or less powdery chips, rather than shaved off in long clean slices.

For roughing out, a gouge ground to a pretty obtuse angle, and held almost at right angles to the work, is generally used when the material belongs to the softer portion of the great hardwood family. For roughing out ivory the point tool is used. It is represented at fig. 57. It is of course used with the beveled side downward, although it is shown in the cut in the reversed position, for the sake of clearness. This remark will apply to all the drawings of hardwood tools.

Figs. 58 and 59 show the form of the right and left side tools. They are used for a variety of purposes, such as trimming up the ends of the work, hollowing out boxes, and so on. If the work in fig. 52 were hardwood, the side tools would be called into requisition. Figs. 60, 61, and 62 give a representation of the inside parting tool, the use of which will be explained further on. They are made with the angle piece at the end of various sizes. There should be at least three of them. The outside parting tools are made from thin flat pieces of steel, slightly hollowed out and ground flat at the cutting edge. The point tool may be used for giving almost any form to the surface of the work, but many amateurs are in the habit of using shaped tools as shown in figs. 65, 66, 67, 68, and 69. The true workman should render himself independent of these aids, and form all his mouldings and hollows with a sharp, keen point tool. By gaining early the necessary skill to design and execute mouldings of various and complicated patterns, he will find his fancy much more unshackled, than if he accustoms himself to the use of tools giving mouldings and hollows of a fixed size and shape.

CHAPTER IV.

FIRST PRACTICE.

HAVING given a very full description of the hand-turning lathe, and the tools to be employed with it, we will now suppose the amateur to have bought and set up his lathe, and to have laid in a stock of tools. He will also require a few saws, a mallet, two or three hammers, a small chopper, an old chisel or two, and a spokeshave for smoothing down the work before putting it into the lathe. A jack-plane and half a dozen gimblets and brad-awls will complete his assortment of ordinary carpenter's tools.

For special use with the lathe he will require a set square, a pair of compasses, a pair of inside and outside callipers for taking diameters and thicknesses, and an oil-can.

The engineer's square (fig. 70) consists of a flat steel rule, generally marked with inches graduated to sixteenths, upon which slides a piece of brass or gun-metal at right angles to the sides of the rule. It is fixed in the desired position either with a screw or else by means of a strong spring inside. It is used for a great variety of purposes, such as for testing the squareness of the ends of your work, measuring the depth of the interior of boxes, &c.

Fig. 71 is an oil-can. It is simply a tin cone with a nozzle screwing off and on, and pierced with a fine hole. The bottom is made of very thin metal, and is slightly convex. It is used by lifting it with the first and second finger placed just under the nozzle, the thumb being underneath ready to press the slightly flexible bottom when necessary. By reversing the cone, and squeezing the bottom slightly with the thumb, a small stream of oil is ejected from the nozzle. The best lubricant for lathe purposes is neat's foot oil, which may be obtained at the tool shops. It has the property of remaining liquid without clogging for a longer period than any other in common use.

Fig. 72 represents a pair of double callipers, or in-and-out callipers, as they are generally called; they are so made that when open the ends a and b are the same distance apart as c and d. The screw at e ought to work rather stiffly, so that in gauging a cylinder or hollowed out spaces, the arms may retain their proper distance apart. Some turners prefer to have separate callipers for measuring inside and outside work, but the amateur will find the double pair the most convenient.

Some soft cotton rag, a stiff brush for cleaning the lathe from chips, and a few sheets of fine glass paper will complete the amateur's equipment.

In commencing work the first thing to do is to examine all the bearings and centres of the lathe, especially the points or friction wheels upon which the crank axle runs. As a rule all centres should be looked to every day before beginning work. There are two faults in the management of centres and bearings that most amateurs are very prone to commit, namely, screwing them up too tightly and oiling them too much. The first will speedily put the parts out of truth, the second is wasteful, slovenly, and unnecessary. Little and often should be the rule for oiling.

Having satisfied yourself that every part of the lathe is clean and in proper working condition, you must first practise with the treadle until you succeed in setting the whole in rapid motion with either foot, without moving the upper part of the body. This sounds an easy thing to do, but except the amateur has been used to working a treadle, he will find it more difficult than he would imagine. The consequence of moving the upper part of the body every time the treadle is pressed, is to cause a corresponding advance in the tool that is being used, and a consequent irregularity in the work.

The next thing will be to take a piece of dry pine or willow, about ten inches long and two inches thick. Work it roughly into a cylinder with an ordinary chisel or spokeshave, taking care to saw off the ends as square as possible. With a pair of compasses mark the centre of each end as accurately as you can. Screw the prong-chuck (figs. 12, 13, and 14) on the lathe, and press upon it the rough cylinder, taking care that the prong is inserted exactly in the centre you have marked with the compasses. The prong of the chuck should enter the wood sufficiently deep for the side edges just to come into play. Holding the cylinder in your left hand, bring the sliding poppet-head with its centre within a quarter of an inch of the centre of the work. Screw up the poppet-head from beneath so that it is perfectly fast and immoveable, and by means of the screw advance the centre so that it enters the wood about the eighth of an inch. You now have your rough cylinder mounted in the lathe. You may, if you like, just touch the back centre with oil to ensure perfect freedom of rotation.

Move the rest to within half an inch of the work, and screw all up tight, taking great care that the rest is parallel to the surface of the work, and a little above the line of its axis. Then with the gouge rough off as much of the surface as you find necessary to bring the work to the state of a perfect cylinder. The gouge must be moved along carefully and firmly, in a straight line, taking off as little as possible each time. Having satisfied yourself that your work is pretty true by the eye, proceed to test it with the callipers. It may here be noticed that, unlike ordinary compasses, callipers are altered by tapping the inside or outside of the legs on the lathe bed. You will possibly find that your first attempt to form a perfect cylinder is a failure, that one end is smaller than the other, or that the centre is larger than either. You must not be discouraged at this, for it is only what every turner has had to put up with at first. If you find your cylinder out of truth, measure the smallest part with the callipers, and reduce the rest to that size. When you find that the cylinder is almost true from end to end, proceed to smooth it down with the chisel, taking care to work as much as possible with the *half of the tool that is nearest to the obtuse angle*. If you attempt at first to even touch the work with the sharp point, you will infallibly dig into the wood, and either break the chisel, spoil the work, or throw the cylinder out of the lathe. Having made a cylinder to your satisfaction, you next proceed to face up the ends, using the obtuse angle of the chisel to finish up with. You will find squaring up almost as difficult as making a perfect cylinder, especially at the chuck end of the work, and it will be only by using the square continually that you will succeed. It is hardly necessary to warn you to be careful in leaving sufficient waste stuff for the work to run upon at each end. These waste pieces are carefully removed with a fine saw after the work is finished. In squaring up the ends, you will find a great difficulty in keeping the angle clean and sharp. Even with the greatest care, pieces will chip out. Never mind if they do, pine and willow are both cheap, and you can begin a new cut without any very disastrous consequences. When you find your cylinder is perfectly true from end to end, that the angles are sharp and clean, and that the faces are true and square, you can smooth up the work with a piece of fine glass paper, finishing up with a close handful of the shavings from the wood itself. If you have succeeded in complying with all the conditions we have named, you may congratulate yourself on having passed the first great *pons asinorum* of the art, that of turning a perfect cylinder with square faces and sharp angles.

FIG. 74.

Fig. 73 will give the young workman an idea of the shape to which the rough cylinder is reduced just before sawing off the waste ends. The light line indicates the rough pieces of wood, the black one the nearly-finished work.

In making our cylinder—as the young workman will no doubt have noticed—we have taken no heed of its size, either in length or diameter; our next lesson ought, therefore, to be directed towards gaining some skill in shaping our work to definite dimensions. A child's skittle of the form indicated in fig. 74, in which every part has a definite size, will be an excellent example to begin with. A cylinder is first turned out of a rough piece of pine, or willow, and the length from A to B is marked on it with a parting tool. At the first attempt it would, perhaps, be as well to provide for any little accident to the corners, by making the marks a quarter of an inch farther apart than necessary. The callipers and square must be called into continual requisition, and great care will be needed in turning down the neck of the skittle not to chip the wood. The two hollows in the body of the work may be formed with the parting tool, and filled up while in the lathe with red or black paint. The two mouldings on the neck are semicircular. The learner should design for himself several other skittles of different sizes, working them accurately to scale. He should also, preparatory to commencing with hardwoods, learn to make and fit a box and its cover with accuracy.

Take a piece of willow, or pine, and turn from it a neat cylinder, three inches in diameter, by three in length. Before cutting off the waste ends, cut it almost in two pieces with the parting tool—say an inch from either end. The parting tool should be used with great care, and when the cylinder is cut through to within—say an eighth of an inch—the work should be taken out of the lathe, and the separation completed with a fine saw. The waste ends should also be sawn off. We have now two cylinders, the larger of which will form the box, and the smaller, the lid ; the larger piece is next fixed accurately in the cup chuck, and the inside carefully turned out with the gouge and chisel, the rest being turned round to face the work. The rim of the box where the cover shuts on, is then formed, and the piece for the cover is substituted in its place. No doubt the first time great difficulty will be felt in making the cover fit the box, the chisel somehow or other always taking off a little too much. When this is the case, you must sacrifice the size of your box by turning off the rim and making a fresh one. You can, if you like, ornament your work with V shaped rings, or, if it is thick enough, with mouldings. The bottom should be made slightly concave on the outside, so that it may stand better. When complete, place it in the cup chuck once more, and finish it up with fine glass paper, and its own shavings.

Having succeeded so far, it is only fair to suppose that the tools you have been using have become blunt, broken, or otherwise rendered unfit for use, we shall therefore pause in our instructions for using the lathe, and devote the next chapter to a description of the best method of keeping tools in order.

CHAPTER V.

SHARPENING TOOLS.

WHEN the tools come from the makers, they are generally in a half blunt condition, except the manufacturer has received special orders from the purchaser to have them properly set and sharpened. It will, therefore, be a good plan for the beginner to have his tools properly sharpened at starting by a competent workman, that he may see what a really sharp tool is.

It is hardly possible to over-estimate the value of keeping one's tools in a perfectly sharp condition. If the skill of the carpenter is known by the neatness of his chips, the turner's ability may be estimated with still greater certainty by a glance at the shavings that have come from his work. At the very beginning the amateur must accustom himself never under any circumstances to work with a blunt or notched tool. A keen, well-set chisel will cut through the work with rapidity and truth, leaving a natural smoothness and polish on the wood which no amount of glass-papering can imitate, whereas a blunt or notched instrument is not only much slower in its action, but the round is generally untrue and rough. If one side of the wood happens to be harder than the other, the blunt tool will naturally act less upon it than on the softer portion, causing a corresponding deviation from the circular form.

The young workman should make it an absolute rule never to begin work without giving his tools a touch on the oilstone.

In sharpening a chisel or other turning tool, there are two distinct operations to be gone through. First, the primary bevel giving the shape to the tool is formed on the grindstone, after which a secondary bevel is produced by a Turkey or other oilstone.

Fig. 74, which is an enlarged diagram of a soft wood chisel, will illustrate this. The bevels in the direction $a\ b$ and $c\ d$ are formed by the grindstone, whilst the others following the lines $e\,f$ and $g\,h$ are those given by the oilstone. Figs. 75 and 76 show the same thing in the case of tools for harder woods and ivory.

The primary bevel is formed by holding the tool perfectly steady, against a revolving grindstone, taking the greatest care not to alter the angle at which it is held. The slightest deviation will cause a new face to be formed, and finally, instead of having a flat, or if the grindstone is small, a slightly concave bevel, an irregularly rounded surface is formed, which cannot be properly set, and will never produce a clean cut. The hands must be moved from side to side as the bevel is formed, otherwise one portion of the grindstone will be worn more than another. It is during this traversing motion that it is most difficult to keep the tool at the proper angle, however practice with soft iron in the first instance will soon enable the learner to produce a clean flat bevel. There is also great danger of moving the tool on its own axis, and so producing rounded corners to it instead of sharp ones.

FIG. 75.

FIG. 76.

FIG. 77.

The grindstone is too familiar an object to need much description. They are generally mounted so as to dip into a trough of water, but they should never be allowed to remain in it, as the part immersed would become softened, and either break or wear away unequally. A grindstone should never be used dry, as it would not only give the tool a rough edge, but there might be sufficient heat generated to soften the steel and destroy its temper.

Grindstones are made from a sharp gritty sandstone found in different parts of England. They are generally turned by a winch, and in most cases should revolve *against* the tool, and not away from it. They are also fitted with a treadle, but we should strongly advise our young friends to purchase one with a winch that can be worked by any companion that may happen to be near, as it leaves both hands and feet at perfect liberty.

The great point in holding the tool steady is to press the arms and elbows well against the sides, the rest of the body being kept firm and motionless.

Having succeeded in making a perfectly flat bevel of the proper angle, it only remains to form the secondary bevel on the oilstone. The best stone for this purpose is the white or black Turkey stone, a close compact mineral found in the interior of Asia Minor. The black variety is slightly harder than the white.

The tool should be held perfectly steady, and passed over the stone some twenty or thirty times. The same difficulty arises here that we met with at the grindstone, that of keeping the tool at the proper angle and producing a single flat bevel instead of several running into each other. The amount of secondary bevel to be given to the tool is very slight. In figs. 74, 75, and 76 it is necessarily much exaggerated, in order to make matters plainer. The tools shown in figs. 67, 68, and 69 are sharpened with a slip of oilstone applied to them in the manner of a file. They are very difficult to keep in order, and we repeat our advice to our readers to exclude them from their stock of tools. The inside of the bevel of the hook tool is sharpened in this way. It will be hardly necessary to warn the amateur against leaving his oilstones uncovered when not in use, as they soon become covered with gritty particles. It is, however, a very common practice to do so.

Oilstones are always let into a solid piece of mahogany or other strong wood, a cover of the same material being hollowed out to fit the stone. A few sharp pins are sometimes driven into the bottom of the block containing the stone, so that it may be fixed immovably on the bench while being used.

Besides black and white Turkey stone, there are several others that may be used, but for giving a fine edge, there is nothing equal to Turkey stone. Arkansas resembles it greatly, but it is more irregular in its texture. Charnley Forest stone, Water of Ayr stone, and Welsh hones belong to the slate family, and are consequently much softer than either Turkey or Arkansas.

Very fine tools are sometimes sharpened in the lathe on a lap or disk of metal composed of lead with a tenth part of antimony melted with it, to give it hardness. It is generally mounted on a brass chuck, the grinding material being fine emery powder mixed into a stiff paste with tallow, and smeared on its surface. The tools are held against the face, being easily kept steady on the rest at any angle that may be necessary. In using it, great care must be taken that none of the sharpening paste drops on any of the working parts of the lathe, or they will wear unequally.

Some very particular turners finish their tools on a strop rubbed with emery powder and tallow, but this is hardly necessary except for any fine work.

CHAPTER VI.

HARDWOOD TURNING.

ONE of the first things the amateur ought to do as soon as he has gained moderate proficiency in his art, is to make himself a set of tool handles. Those sold at the shops are generally mounted in beech, but the harder woods are more proper for the purpose. The other day the author saw a set of tools mounted in first-rate style by an amateur turner who had only been at work for a week or ten days. The handles were all made to the same pattern, but the woods for each class of tool were different, so that when they were lying about the bench, a particular chisel or gouge could be found at once. Thus the gouges were all mounted in box, the chisels in rosewood, the parting tools in walnut, and so on.

The first thing to do is to procure a piece of stout brass tube about half or three-quarters of an inch in diameter. A length of this is driven on to a piece of pine or beech that has been turned in the lathe to fit it. The whole is then mounted between the centres, the centre chuck, figs. 9 and 10, and the carrier, fig. 33, being used for the purpose. The tube is next cut into rings about a half or three-quarters of an inch wide with the hardwood point tool or a triangular file, ground down to a cutting point, and, if necessary, they may be brightened with emery paper. These brass rings serve the purpose of ferules, and are driven on the upper part of the handle, to prevent it being split when the tool is driven in. It would be as well to make two or three dozen of these rings, as they are useful. A piece of wood—box is the best to begin upon—having been chosen, the centre chuck is replaced by the prong chuck, and a small portion of the end nearest the mandril is turned down to fit the ferules. The body of the handle is then turned to any shape the amateur may like to use. It will be excellent practice to turn several different patterns at first, and find out for himself which one fits his hand the best.

If the young workman has practised much with soft wood he will find it rather difficult at first to adapt the position of his tool to the material he is at work upon; indeed, in the trade it is very seldom that we find a workman excelling both in hard and soft wood turning, the treatment of the two classes of material in the lathe being so different. If it is a piece of boxwood he is at work upon, he will find that the inequalities in the rough piece will continually drive his tool from its position. This must be remedied by firmly grasping the boss of the hand rest with the left hand, and holding the tool tightly in its place with the thumb. Box being of medium hardness, the angle at which the tool is ground should not be too obtuse.

When finished, the work should be smoothed with a piece of fine glass paper, made finer as the process proceeds by being rubbed against another piece. The finishing touch is given with a rag very slightly moistened with linseed oil. Some turners use a piece of waxed cloth, wetted with a few drops of turpentine, but if the tools used have been properly sharpened, very little artificial polishing will be necessary.

Tool handles are of various lengths, those for soft wood being often as long as fifteen or eighteen inches, but hardwood tools do not require their handles to be longer than eight or nine inches. The young workman should begin with the short ones, as they are the easiest to turn. If the pattern is at all complicated, it will be well to make what is called a *template*. The pattern is cut out in section from a piece of sheet zinc or tin, and used to test the truth with which the worker adheres to his pattern; it is a good plan to rub the edges of the template with chalk, so that when it is applied to the work, the prominent portions which require reduction may be more easily discovered.

The amateur should next set to work to make himself a series of boxwood chucks for holding the different objects that he may have to turn, and which will not fit in the cup-chuck.

When he buys the lathe he should provide himself with a set of screw taps for making hollow screws of the same size as that on the nose of the mandril. A piece of boxwood of suitable dimensions is then placed on the screw chuck, fig. 15, and turned to a cylindrical form, the end being carefully squared, a hole is next made in the centre of the flat portion, and with the parting tool, the hand-rest being turned round to face the work. The hole should be of such a size as to admit the small end of the smallest screw-tap. The work is then removed from the lathe and fixed in the vice with the hole upwards. The formation of a thread with the screw-tap is a very simple operation. The smallest is inserted in the hole to be screwed, and turned round by means of the handle, a slight downward pressure being given at the same time. It is of course evident that the tap must be kept perfectly upright, or the screw will be crooked. When the smallest tap has reached the bottom of the hole, the two others should be used to complete the screw, when it is finished it should be fixed on the nose of the mandril, and a hole, say an inch in diameter, cut in its face, the sides and bottom of the hole being made very square and true. Half-a-dozen of these, with holes of different sizes, varying from half an inch to three inches in diameter, should be made, the holes being afterwards enlarged to fit the work. Fig. 18 is an excellent form for a boxwood cup-chuck.

Having provided himself with a set of tool handles in rosewood, walnut, and box, the amateur may next try his hand at something harder, for instance, a piece of sound black ebony. A snuff box will make a very good object for first practice. Ebony is one of the hardest woods we possess, almost rivalling ivory in its closeness of grain and susceptibility of polish.

A suitable piece having been chosen, it may be worked into a rough cylindrical form with an old chisel or gouge, and inserted in a boxwood chuck. The end to the right must be turned perfectly cylindrical and square, making its diameter a shade larger than three inches. Another chuck is now inserted in its place, and a hole turned in it to fit the finished end of the ebony cylinder exactly. The rough end is next completed, and the piece for the cover cut off. When we were working in willow and pine, it will be remembered that we reduced the inside of our box to a mass of shavings, but with a hard wood like ebony this would take a long time, besides being very wasteful. The following method of removing the interior of the box is the simplest and easiest.

Having decided on the depth of the box, you cut a groove with a pointed parting tool almost to the lowest point. You then insert the smallest of the square-headed inside parting tools (fig. 62), cutting away with it as far as it will go. The second size is then used, after that the third, and so on until the piece drops out. The figures 79, 80, and

FIG. 79. FIG. 80.

81 will illustrate this. If the box is too broad for the largest inside parting tool, a hole may be made in the middle to allow of its being used both ways. Fig. 82 will illustrate this. If the cover is too shallow to need being cut out without wasting the central piece, the

interior may be removed in chips. The rest of the work is performed in the same manner as when working in willow.

When the young turner has so far conquered his work as to be able to produce almost any form he pleases, he should commence working in ivory. Ivory, as he will soon find out, is a very expensive material, and, consequently, not well adapted for trial work. One of his first essays in ivory turning ought to be a sphere. He begins by making a cylinder, whose diameter is exactly equal to its length. The middle of the cylinder should be marked with a very fine red line—a little vermillion water-colour is, perhaps, the best material for the purpose. The centres

Fig. 81.   Fig. 82.

of the ends should also be marked with a small dot in the same manner. A semi-circular template should next be cut out of a piece of tin plate, and its edge slightly smeared with a little lampblack and oil. The cylinder being fixed with perfect truth in the boxwood cup chuck, the corners are carefully and slowly turned down, the template being constantly applied as the work advances. The greatest care must be taken not to efface the red marks. When you have turned one hemisphere to your liking, reverse the work. You will find some difficulty in centreing it properly in this instance, for the part that fits into the chuck is no longer cylindrical but spherical, the hold, consequently, that the chuck has upon it is extremely slight. You will now see the use of the red dots at each end of the cylinder, and it will only be by great patience and very gentle taps that you will be able to centre your work. If the chuck is slightly chalked, you will find it hold the ivory better. If you succeed in making your ball truly spherical in every direction at the first, or even the sixth trial, you may congratulate yourself on doing what very few amateurs ever accomplish. It sounds very easy when described, but in practice it is very difficult, and the amateur who can turn an ivory or hard-wood ball with even a moderate degree of exactitude may call himself a very clever turner.

Cutting male and female screws in hard wood and ivory is the next branch of the art of turning to which the young workman ought to apply himself.

There are two kinds of screws, male and female, or external and internal. Thus the thread cut on a bolt is a male or external screw, that formed on the inside of the nut is the female or internal screw. Screws are formed in two ways, either by the use of taps and dies, or in the lathe by screw-cutting tools. As screws are rarely formed on ivory or hard wood by taps and dies, it will be as well to leave our description of them until we come to metal turning. The formation of a female screw by means of a tap has been already briefly described when treating of boxwood chucks at the beginning of this chapter, but it will be much better if the amateur will procure for himself a screw-cutting tool to fit the threads on the nose of the mandril, and form his screws in the lathe instead of by means of taps. Figs. 83 and 84 are screw-tools for internal and external work. They are made by pressing a piece of soft steel against a master tap revolving on a lathe, the master tap being a hard steel screw, with longitudinal grooves cut in it, so as to form sharp cutting edges. A counterpart of the screw is soon formed on the tool, which is afterwards hardened, tempered, and sharpened, by being ground upon its face.

Fig. 83.   Fig. 84.

The action of these tools is as follows:—

The cylinder or hollow upon which the screw-thread is to be formed is fixed in the lathe in the most convenient way, and the screw-tool held gently against it. The teeth of the tool, which are slightly askew, cut a continuous spiral groove on the surface of the work, which will be an exact counterpart of the original screw from which the tool was formed. The great benefit to be gained in using the screw-tool is, that you can form a thread upon outside or inside work of any diameter, whereas when using taps and dies the diameter must be in all cases identical.

It is somewhat difficult at first to start a thread cleanly. The screw-tool is held steadily, but not too firmly, on the rest at the right hand end of the part to be screwed. The lathe should be worked somewhat slowly, and the tool advanced very gently. As soon as the tool touches the work, it should be traversed from right to left, so as to follow up the spiral made by its teeth. The spiral line formed at first should be the merest scratch, and as soon as it is made examine it minutely, to see if it is perfectly regular. If it is not turn it out and try another. If, however, the spiral is regular, increase its depth with the screw-tool to the desired amount. The inside screw-tool is used precisely in the same manner. There is a peculiar knack in using the screw-tool that is very difficult to describe intelligibly. In fact, it is as hard to put into words as the way of making leg-hits at cricket, both operations being most easily learned by a practical lesson or two.

It is a very great advantage to the amateur turner to be able to use the screw-tool with ease, for it often happens that articles are much more easily made in several pieces which can be afterwards screwed together, than when cut out of the solid piece. Box-lids, needle-case covers, and a thousand-and-one other articles are much better adapted to the use for which they are intended, when they screw and unscrew, than when they simply shut.

Another great advantage of being a good screw-cutter is the ease with which chucks of all shapes and sizes may be constructed. Screw-tools are sharpened by rubbing their *upper* surfaces on the oilstone, they seldom require grinding as the wear and tear upon them is comparatively small.

CHAPTER VII.

ON THE CHOICE OF MATERIALS.

THE amateur having gained tolerable proficiency in the use of the lathe, will naturally next begin to look about for raw materials, upon which to exercise his skill, of a more varied character than those we have already enumerated. The class of woods will furnish him with an almost inexhaustible supply of all degrees of hardness and toughness, and of great variety of colour.

It is much to be regretted that, as a rule, amateurs are too fond of confining themselves to ivory, box, ebony, and cocoa, forgetting, or perhaps not knowing of the existence of such beautiful materials as kingwood, camwood, partridge-wood, and a host of others. They also seem to strive as much as possible to form their work out of a single piece of ivory or ebony, as the case may be, instead of making the different parts of woods of various colours. The reason of this may be sought in the fact that so few amateurs have learned the use of the screw-tool. The ambitious young workman should turn his attention seriously to this part of the subject, and show his friends that he can not only produce good work with his tools and lathe, but also artistic form and pleasing combinations of colour with his head and eye. The following list of woods, with their characteristic tints and markings, will be of great help to him in this.

Apple-tree.—This is a close-grained yellowish wood, with a reddish tinge, of moderate toughness. It is much used for bottle-cases and screwed work, but is inferior for those purposes to pear-tree, which is closer and harder in grain. It should not be used for any very large work, as it is liable to cast. As a reddish-yellow wood, it may be used for ornamental purposes with great advantage.

Beech.—This tree is found abundantly in most countries of Europe. The Buckingham and Sussex wood is considered the best in England. It is very even in its texture, is moderately tough, and is much used for tool handles and chucks. From not being very hard, it is inferior to box for these purposes.

Beefwood.—This name is given to several woods grown in different parts of the world. The principal supply is obtained from New South Wales, where it is known as the Botany Bay oak. It is of a fine reddish-brown colour, with dark curly veins running through it. It is hard, close, and compact, and is greatly used for ornamental purposes.

Birch.—Birchwood is grown abundantly in Europe and North America. That from Canada is considered the best. It is softer than beech. Its colour is sometimes very beautiful, especially the variety grown in Russia, which is of a rich yellow.

Boxwood.—The finest quality of this wood is grown in the interior of Turkey, and on the shores of the Black Sea. It forms one of the principal exports from Smyrna to this country, and is in great request for wood-engraving and other purposes. When cut across the grain, it will take the finest lines from the graver without chipping. It is hard, close, and compact, of a fine yellow colour, and capable of receiving a high polish. It is frequently very beautifully mottled, and should form one of the principal woods of the amateur's stock for both useful and ornamental purposes. For tool-handles and chucks it is invaluable. For the latter purposes, the English wood may be employed, as it is tough, and its fibre is more elastic than the Turkish variety. Its sawdust is used for cleaning jewellery.

Bullet-wood.—This is a close, hard, and regular wood, and would be very valuable, if it could be obtained in larger quantities, being well adapted for the lathe. The West Indian variety is of a greenish brown that from Berbice inclining more to hazel.

Cam-wood is grown in the country surrounding Sierra Leone, and on other parts of the West African coast. It is fine, close, and hard, of a bright orange-brown streaked with red. It is generally very beautifully marked at first, but in course of time it becomes much darker,—a remark that will apply to most woods of a very bright colour.

Cherry-tree.—A moderately hard, close-grained, reddish-brown wood, When soaked in lime-water, it takes the colour and appearance of mahogany.

Cocoa or *Cocos-wood.*—This wood has nothing to do either with the cocoa-nut palm or the cacao tree, from which the cocoa nib is obtained. It is hard, close, and compact, at first of a dark brown, afterwards turning almost to black. It is greatly used for very fine work, as it is less liable to chip under the tool than almost any other wood.

Coromandel wood is very hard, of a deep chocolate-brown, with black veins and streaks running through it, and resembles ebony in working and quality.

Ebony.—The intense blackness of this well-known wood has given rise to the common simile, "as black as ebony." That from Mauritius is the hardest, finest, and blackest; but it is frequently full of shakes and cracks. The East Indian variety, which is obtained from India, Ceylon, and the East Indian islands, is superior in point of soundness, but is coarser, softer, and less black, whilst the African wood from the Cape of Good Hope is the least wasteful of all, but is the most porous and worst in depth of colour. *Green Ebony* is the wood of an entirely different tree growing in the West Indies. It is of a greenish-brown, streaked irregularly with black, and, except in small pieces, is not much employed in ornamental turning. It is much used for making round rulers.

Holly.—This well-known wood should form the amateur's *pièce de résistance*, whenever he requires a light-coloured material. The best specimens are of a rich creamy white, moderately hard, close and fine-grained. Although somewhat soft, it takes a beautiful natural polish. and is much less liable to pick up dust and dirt than horse-chestnut, sycamore, and other white woods.

Horse-chestnut is a white, close, soft, silky-grained wood, but it will not replace holly for ornamental purposes.

King-wood, or *Violet-wood.*—This magnificently-marked wood truly deserves the name of king-wood. It is pretty hard, has a fine close grain, and is beautifully streaked with different shades of violet. As a means of introducing colour into ornamental work, it is perhaps unequalled.

Kiabooca-wood, or *Amboyna-wood,* as it is often termed, is another ornamental wood, which for beauty of colour may vie with king-wood. It varies from orange to reddish-brown, and is beautifully marked with curly streaks. Few other woods exceed it in beauty, more especially when large flat surfaces are exposed to view.

Pear-tree is similar to apple-tree, but is somewhat browner, tougher, and less liable to cast. It is much used for printing-blocks, as it cuts with great facility in all directions of the grain.

Purple-wood is said to be a variety of king-wood. When worked it is of a dark grey, which gradually turns to a deep purple.

Partridge-wood is another material that is highly esteemed for ornamental purposes. It is close, heavy, and straight-grained. The markings are brown of various shades, streaked with grey; and some specimens bear a singular resemblance to the feathers of the bird from which it is named.

Lignum Vitæ is a hard, heavy wood, used greatly for skittle-balls, tops, rollers, sheaves for ships' blocks, and other coarse work of a similar character. It is of a dull greenish-brown in colour, and is too irregular in tint and grain to be used in ornamental turning.

Mahogany is too familiar to need description. The Spanish variety is more close-grained and hard than that from Honduras, besides being generally beautifully marked.

Maple.—The American variety of this wood—generally called bird's-eye maple—forms an excellent material for large works. It is too well known to need description.

Quassia-wood is sometimes turned into cups, which give out the bitter principle of the wood when water is poured into them. It is a soft wood, and destitute of ornamental qualities.

Red Sanders-wood is hard and heavy. It has a fine red colour at first, but afterwards turns brown.

Rosetta-wood is of a bright-red orange, streaked with dark veins. At first it is very beautiful, but gradually becomes darker.

Rose-wood is hard and close in most specimens; there are many logs, however, which are comparatively soft. It is not an easy wood to turn smooth, owing to the dark portions being harder than the rest. It is used both for furniture and turned work in large quantities. The best quality comes from Rio de Janeiro. It contains a fragrant oil, which is exceedingly inflammable, a small splinter of the wood burning like a candle.

Sandal-wood is the product of a myrtle-like tree growing in Malabar It is a yellow wood, somewhat resembling box in appearance, but is much softer. It ought to be a great favourite with the amateur, on account of the delicious perfume it constantly exhales.

Satin-wood is of a fine yellow colour, close-grained and moderately hard. It turns well in the lathe, with care. Some specimens are beautifully mottled.

Snake-wood.—This wood is of a bright brown colour, splashed with darker brown or black spots; whence its name. It is rather scarce and dear in this country.

Tulip-wood is a favourite ornamental material with the cabinet-maker and turner. It is of a light reddish-brown, with blood-red streaks. It is difficult to work in the lathe, being splintery and apt to chip. It is best adapted to work with broad surfaces.

Yacca-wood is pale brown, streaked with hazel.

Zebra- or *Pigeon-wood* is orange-brown, streaked with dark brown. It is very handsome, and not difficult to work.

Besides the woods above mentioned, the turner uses ivory, bone, horn, and shells and nuts, of various kinds.

In point of beauty, the chief of these is undoubtedly ivory. In all ages, and in all countries where true art has flourished, we find this beautiful substance extensively used.

Ivory is the hard substance forming the tusks of the male elephant, walrus, and sea-horse. They are hollow at the root, and vary in size according to the age of the animal. The finest quality is imported in large quantities from the west and east coasts of Africa. The East Indian ivory, the product of Ceylon and the continent of India, is of inferior quality, being less close in texture, and more liable to turn brown than that from Africa.

Horn and bone being rarely used by the amateur, need no particular description.

The betel-nut is much used for small work, such as the knobs of parasols, the covers of small boxes, and similar articles. It is the product of the *Areca catechu*, a graceful palm which grows extensively in the tropics. The main body of the nut is of a greyish-white, covered with bright brown markings, which form a pretty network over the whole surface. The betel-nut is rather softer than ivory, and about the size of a small walnut.

The Coquilla-nut is the fruit of the *Attalea funifera*, a tree growing principally in Brazil. It contains two seeds, which taste something like cocoa-nut. It is of bright yellowish-brown, streaked with lighter and darker markings. It bears a high polish, and, being hard and tough, forms excellent screws.

The Corosos, or Vegetable Ivory nuts, are the product of the *Phytelephas macrocarpa*, a native of Central America. They are of an irregular globular shape, and contain a hole in the middle. They are whiter than ivory, but in course of time they become dusky in hue. They are hard and tough, screw well, and take a high polish.

Ivory and the nuts generally should be finished with a rag covered with whiting. A finishing touch with an infinitesimal portion of oil may be given; but in the case of ivory too much is liable to turn it yellow.

THE END OF THE LATHE, AND HOW TO USE IT.

www.ingramcontent.com/pod-product-compliance
Lightning Source LLC
Chambersburg PA
CBHW070536010526
44118CB00012B/1143